TRANSPERSONAL BOOKS

James Fadiman, *General Editor*

Transpersonal Books explore the psychology of consciousness
and possibilities for transcendence
through altered states of consciousness,
paranormal phenomena, spiritual disciplines,
and other modes of extended awareness

GAY HENDRICKS is an assistant professor in the School of Education,
University of Colorado, Colorado Springs.
He is the author, with Russel Wills,
of *The Centering Book* (Prentice-Hall).

JAMES FADIMAN is a lecturer
in the Department of Mechanical Engineering,
Stanford University,
and former president
of the Association for Transpersonal Psychology.
He has written and edited several books
on transpersonal psychology.

TRANSPERSONAL EDUCATION

A Curriculum for Feeling and Being

Edited by

GAY HENDRICKS

JAMES FADIMAN

A SPECTRUM BOOK

PRENTICE-HALL, INC., ENGLEWOOD CLIFFS, NEW JERSEY

Library of Congress Cataloging in Publication Data
MAIN ENTRY UNDER TITLE:

Transpersonal education.

   (Transpersonal books)   (A Spectrum Book)
   Bibliography: p.
   1. Creative thinking (Education)   2. Imagination.
3. Psychical research and children.   I. Hendricks, Gay.
II. Fadiman, James, (date)
LB1062.T72   370.15 '3   76-15235
ISBN 0-13-930479-7
ISBN 0-13-930461-4 pbk.

For Amanda, Susan, Stephen,
and the children of the future.   G.H.

For my daughters Renee and Maria,
who remind me that learning is joy

For my wife Dorothy, who understands.   J.F.

   The figures on pages 125 and 147 were adapted from *Bioenergetics* by Alexander Lowen, M.D. Copyright © 1975 by Alexander Lowen, M.D. They are used by permission of Coward, McCann & Geoghegan, Inc. and the author.

10   9   8   7   6   5   4   3   2   1

PRENTICE-HALL INTERNATIONAL, INC. (*London*)
PRENTICE-HALL OF AUSTRALIA PTY. LTD. (*Sydney)*
PRENTICE-HALL OF CANADA LTD. (*Toronto*)
PRENTICE-HALL OF INDIA PRIVATE LIMITED (*New Delhi*)
PRENTICE-HALL OF JAPAN, INC. (*Tokyo*)
PRENTICE-HALL OF SOUTHEAST ASIA PTE. LTD. (*Singapore*)

Contents

Preface

Are you one of those teachers who is always on the lookout for something new to bring to the classroom? If so, read on.

Are you a parent, a principal, or a professor who thinks it is still possible to generate real excitement in school? If so, this may be your book.

We believe that learning is the natural state in children and that when children are learning things of interest to them, there is ease and delight in the process. Unfortunately, the ease and delight of learning begin to decline when the child enters a school setting where the whole person is not developed. Human beings are whole beings, with cognitive, social, emotional, and spiritual potentials. Transpersonal education *is* education for the whole person, and views the school as a place where this wholeness can be supported and encouraged.

It is the primary task of the teacher to maintain and strengthen the child's basic urge toward further learning. Although many people embrace this position philosophically, most schools continue to be places where the natural urge for learning is stunted, places where learning becomes a chore. Such schools have shown that it is possible to dampen children's spontaneous enthusiasm for any area of the curriculum.

There is a saying from the Middle East: "He who tastes knows." This book is about ways to help students get more of the taste of their own education, to make the classroom experience more alive. Transpersonal education helps students gain more control of their capacity to learn, so that they can expand the ways in which they understand and appreciate the objective content which is still the core of the curriculum. In addition, transpersonal education suggests a new set of activities for the classroom, activities aimed at the development of the whole person.

The papers assembled here are part of an emerging point of view which is beginning to allow greater freedom and flexibility in education. Many of the writers are practical, determined educators who, in their quest for new approaches, are incorporating practices from a dozen fields into the teaching/learning situation. Insights gained from the upsurge of interest in meditation, biofeedback, martial arts, Eastern thought, and altered states of consciousness are finding their ways into the classroom. Stripped of their jargon, these fields of study are accelerating and improving conventional learning, as well as bringing new and more personal areas of learning into the classroom.

Transpersonal education is not revolutionary (we've had enough "revolutions" in education), and it is not the ultimate solution to all our educational problems. But because it is a source of powerful new tools and possibilities for the classroom, teachers like it, and students are excited when they find that the ideas of transpersonal education are not limited to subject matter but have extensive transfer into their personal lives.

Part I of the book is an introduction to the scope of the transpersonal point of view. The content of the papers range from the practical (Roberts and Clark, Hendricks) to the visionary (Huxley, Krishnamurti). Upon close reading, however, the reader may find a wealth of practical information in the "visionary" papers, and more than a touch of the visionary in the "practical" papers. This seemingly odd posture—head in the clouds but feet firmly planted in the ground—is a common characteristic of transpersonal educators.

Part II is the how-to-do-it section of the book. Here the reader will find articles on classroom use of dreams, fantasy, biofeedback, psychic abilities, meditation, and other techniques. This section also contains reports from teachers who have used transpersonal techniques successfully in their classrooms.

Part III offers readings which the editors feel capture the essence of transpersonal education at its best. Rather than risk devitalizing these readings through summarization, the editors leave it to the reader to discover the common threads which are woven through these selections.

Finally, there is a list of materials you may eventually want to track down if you continue to expand in these areas.

Charles Darwin was once approached by two small boys, children of a family with whom he was visiting. The boys had caught a butterfly, a centipede, a beetle, and a grasshopper. Taking the centipede's body, the butterfly's wings, the beetle's head, and the grasshopper's legs, they had fashioned an alarming and original insect.

"We caught this bug in the field," they said innocently. "What kind of a bug is it, Mr. Darwin?"

Darwin examined it solemnly. "Did you notice whether it hummed when you caught it, boys?" he asked gravely.

"Yes, sir," they answered, trying to conceal their mirth.

"Just as I thought," said Darwin. "It is a humbug."

A great deal of what goes on in education under the name of "new, exciting solutions" turns out to be humbug. However, many people *are* genuinely excited about the potentials of transpersonal education. We would be pleased if you would try some of the ideas contained herein, filter out the useful from the humbug, and let us know your results.

INTRODUCTION TO TRANSPERSONAL EDUCATION

What is transpersonal education? Although no one has yet successfully defined the term transpersonal, *the authors in this section cover various facets by approaching it from very different angles.*

In his book The Psychology of Consciousness, *Robert Ornstein provides evidence from current brain research that there are two modes of consciousness at work in human beings: one, a rational, logical, and active mode, is associated with the left side of the brain, while the other, a mystical, intuitive, and receptive mode, seems to be the function of the right side of the brain. In a sense, this information is not new, since poets and philosophers have been hinting at this phenomenon for thousands of years; what is remarkable is that science is finding a physical basis for the existence of the two modes.*

These findings have profound implications for education, for it seems clear that our current educational efforts are aimed primarily at the left side of the brain, thereby leaving an entire model of consciousness to chance development. Although their approaches are widely diverse, the authors in this first section agree on one point: transpersonal education is an approach that aims at the concurrent development of the logical and the mystical, the analytical and the intuitive.

Tom Roberts and Frances Clark, in the first article, provide a concise but comprehensive statement of the domain of transpersonal education. Although focusing on the day-to-day use of transpersonal psychology in education, the authors explore the philosophical implications of the transpersonal approach. The second selection, by Aldous Huxley, contains a description of a transpersonal education curriculum that is nearly as radical today as it was when it was written twenty years ago.

The third selection, drawn from the works of the Indian teacher Krishnamurti, speaks for itself, simply and beautifully, and needs no comment from us. The last reading in the section, written by one of the editors, is a practical guide to personalizing and transpersonalizing the classroom.

We hope that through your reading of the following selections you will form your own definition of transpersonal education, and perhaps begin to formulate your own ways of using it.

Transpersonal Psychology in Education

Thomas B. Roberts
Frances V. Clark

What is the scope of transpersonal education? What are its origins? Thomas Roberts and Frances Clark, two pioneering transpersonal educators, provide cogent answers to these and other important questions.

TRANSPERSONAL PSYCHOLOGY

The development of a comprehensive educational psychology requires a theoretical framework which includes all the phenomena related to human learning, and must therefore include areas of human experience which previously have been ignored by traditional academic psychology. Freudian, behavioral, and humanistic psychologies are seen as useful, but incomplete psychologies. Transpersonal psychology offers a more inclusive vision of human potential, suggesting both a new image of man

"Transpersonal Psychology in Education." From Thomas G. Roberts and Frances V. Clark, *Transpersonal Psychology in Education,* Fastback Pamphlet Series, #53 (Bloomington, Indiana: Phi Delta Kappa Educational Foundation, 1975), pp. 7-33. Reprinted by permission of the publisher.

and a new world view. Using transpersonal psychology in education does not require a complete rejection of established educational psychologies, but may be used in conjunction with them. Conflicts occur at some points, and agreement occurs at others.

An underlying assumption of transpersonal psychology is that physical, emotional, intellectual, and spiritual growth are interrelated, and the optimal educational environment simulates and nurtures the intuitive as well as the rational, the imaginative as well as the practical, and the creative as well as the receptive functions of each individual. Transpersonal psychology has focused attention on the human capacity for self-transcendence as well as self-realization, and is concerned with the optimum development of consciousness.

Most topics being investigated by transpersonal psychologists consist of the psychological aspects of at least one of the following: a new image of man and a new world view, altered states of consciousness (including meditation, dreams, etc.), impulses toward higher states (such as peak experiences), self-realization and self-transcendence, subjective experience and inner states, spiritual growth, parapsychology and psychic phenomena, other cultures and their psychologies (especially Eastern psychologies), newly discovered forms of energy, recent physiological research (such as voluntary control of internal states), and evolving consciousness.

Many psychologists judge that we use less than 10 percent of our capacities. Transpersonal psychologists are seeking to increase our understanding of human abilities in order to unlock some of our latent potentials. How can we learn to use some of the abilities which may be hidden in our own minds? A partial answer may be found in studying people who have unusual abilities, and in the cultural, social, and psychological factors affecting their development.

Transpersonal psychology gives us a new perspective on the old Delphic precept, "Know thyself." In turning our attention to the inner world of man, we are indeed discovering a wealth of unsuspected resources. Many of the transpersonal techniques for using inner imagery in the process of self-discovery are well suited to classroom use, and may easily be introduced in the existing educational system. As the universal language of human experience, inner imagery finds expression in all forms of creativity, be it artistic, scientific, or philosophical. As a student becomes familiar with his own inner resources, he develops a new awareness of his individual uniqueness and his relationship to others and the environment. Research in transpersonal psychology has indicated that working with imagery can have a beneficial effect on physical, emotional, mental, and spiritual well-being. It is important that we begin to give students access to these tools that can be used for continuing growth and awareness throughout their lives. In applying transpersonal psychology to education, both students and teachers can assume responsibility for making choices, and develop a sense of inner direction in their lives.

CURRENT CLASSROOM APPLICATIONS

The first step in applying transpersonal psychology to education usually involves shifting the focus from external to internal awareness. As students become aware of their own inner states, they can begin to recognize important conditions which affect their learning ability.

Relaxation and Concentration

Can you remember a time when you were concentrating so intently on something, perhaps a hobby, a sport, or some creative endeavor, that you lost all sense of time and were able to think and act super-efficiently? Or can you remember a time when you were so clearheaded you learned a complex task easily? This state of mind, which occurs spontaneously at random, can also be consciously developed. Although a person's state of mind is a major variable in how well he performs, we seldom teach people to move into an appropriate state of mind before undertaking a task. Investigating such states of mind has been the focus of transpersonal psychologists who are interested in self-induced altered states of consciousness evidenced in psychic healing, parapsychological phenomena, yoga, biofeedback, and meditation. Teaching the voluntary control of internal states is one area of transpersonal psychology which is easily applied to education, and the first step is the introduction of relaxation training. Relaxation training is important both for everyday functioning as a beginning step to more advanced training in meditation and concentration. The immediate effects of relaxation can be experienced both by teachers and students, and many who have tried it find short periods of intensive relaxation to be of considerable benefit.

For example, a German teacher had a class in which the students seemed too keyed up for their own good. "Whenever we would have a Unit Test, always a biggie in their minds, no matter how much I would try to play it down, the tenseness would permeate the classroom." In one unit test, his ten students scored 5 A's, 3 B's, and 2 C's. The following unit test had proved to be more difficult in previous years, so he tried to improve their recall and ability, not by pushing and drilling them harder, but by relaxing them at the time of the test. Here is his report:

Well, I chanced the great experiment. My only worry was the time element. The 48-minute class period was cut to 38 minutes as I darkened the room and played a commercial relaxation tape received from a friend. The students sat in their seats, heads down on their forearms, legs uncrossed; then I took them on and through an original fantasy journey in the German language. This particular part had to be condensed into 8 minutes, because of the time element. With about 28 minutes of time left, the students proceeded to work on the test which usually takes at least 30 to 35 minutes to complete. Observing the students while they were writing and thinking, I detected the total absence of nail-chewing and the usual pencil tapping on the desktops and nervous, quick glances at the clock. Everybody finished the test on time. Grading the test was fun; 7 A's and 3 B's was the obvious result. The quality of writing in some of the usually more sloppy papers improved markedly. The students just could not believe this. It was only after I explained to them that a lot of their learned knowledge was not able to surface because of their nervousness and fear and the tension, and once they were relaxed, the learned storehouse of information was able to be tapped.

Other teachers who have taught their students to relax find similar results. Some students who catch on to the techniques use them to reduce tension in other classes as well as in up-tight social situations when they want to feel more at ease.

These exploratory applications of relaxation training need not be taken as proof that relaxation will automatically improve test scores, but these intriguing findings keep reappearing, and indicate an area where further investigation and experimentation may lead to the development of transpersonal teaching methods. The fact that students are able to improve their recall by controlling their breathing, relaxing their muscles, and learning to direct their own attention exemplifies two important principles: First, our behavior is influenced by *internal* states, and these states can be controlled voluntarily. Second, the mind and body are inextricably connected. When we control one, the other is inevitably affected.

Effective methods of mind/body control have been practiced in yoga for thousands of years, yet we are only beginning to explore the possibilities of mind/body learning. Training in deep relaxation has immediate physical benefits, since it can help people fall asleep quickly and gives the body a chance to revitalize itself in brief periods of time. Some coaches say they have found that it allows their athletes not to waste their energy in pregame nervousness, but to consciously direct their own levels of activity by selecting the right amount of energy for the task at hand. Relaxation is a prime mental/physical ability that people can use daily throughout their lives. As such it certainly deserves a place in the physical education curriculum alongside the rules of badminton and the techniques of wrestling take-downs.

In schools, relaxation is easily combined with concentration. After the students are relaxed, then they can direct their attention toward academic content, or they can let their minds idle in creative association. Aldous Huxley could select his degree of relaxation and breadth of concentration when he worked. If his wife were home, he would not hear the doorbell or telephone, but if she went out, he would hear them. In his "deep reflection," as he called it, he had almost perfect recall. Probably everybody has had instances of becoming so involved in reading or working that he temporarily forgets himself, and then is able to remember or accomplish much more than usual. Perhaps we would all learn to do this at will, maybe not as well as Aldous Huxley, maybe better. The challenge to education is: Can we learn to do this so that we can do it whenever we want? Can we teach others to do it too?

Guided Fantasy

One method of facilitating concentration and directing attention is guided fantasy. Specifically, directed fantasy trips are useful for learning specific content, while open-ended fantasies evoke creativity and aid self-discovery. The following example illustrates the use of guided fantasy as an aid to learning content in an electronics class.

I took my beginning electronics class on a fantasy trip into that mysterious land of invisible magnetic and electric fields surrounding the windings and core of a transformer. The procedure was as follows. The room was darkened and everyone put their heads down on the desks and were told to relax and empty their minds. Prior to beginning the journey a relaxation exercise was performed. Everyone was told to imagine themselves as an electron and to concentrate on what it might feel like to be such an incredibly small piece of (negatively charged) matter. They were to encounter two very large coils of wire, and around the wire there was a huge and rapidly changing force field. They were to enter the force field and feel the effects of it. They were then told to enter the wire of the coil and experience the movement of the rest of the electrons within the coil of wire as they were affected by the rapidly changing force field, which is the electromagnetic field. I told the students that another coil of equal size and strength was coming toward them. The two fields were interacting, and the interaction became very violent the closer the coils came to each other. The students were told that the increase in strength of one coil caused an increase in the strength of the other coil. This produced a super-strong force which moved the electrons (students) very fast.

(After a waking period, the teacher turned on a small light and discussed the experience with them.)

The next day the students read the chapter in the book dealing with inductive coils. The students said they had no trouble visualizing the forces described in the book, and other qualitative work in the lab seemed to bear this out. It is quite evident to me that the trip was worth taking since I have taught this subject matter before but not with this much success.

Teachers who have used the fantasy journeys hold a key to improved instruction: less stimulation, not more, and temporary escape from the stimulus overload of a hectic, rushing world of school halls and ringing bells.

Why do fantasy journeys work? This is a good question for educational researchers. Recent speculations of neurophysiologists studying the brain suggest that the left hemisphere of the brain thinks in words and clearly defined symbols such as chemical and mathematical symbols. It is active, calculating, reasoning, and is predominantly sequential and analytic in its functioning. The right hemisphere, on the other hand, is spatially oriented, thinks in pictures, perceives patterns as a whole, and operates in an intuitive, emotional, and receptive mode.

Although the "sideness" of mental functions is highly speculative because it is based on split-brain research, Robert Ornstein's metaphorical use of "right-function" and "left-function" is relevant to educators. According to researcher Ornstein:

It is the polarity and the integration of these two modes of consciousness, the complementary workings of the intellect and the intuitive, which underlie our highest achievements.

Most of our education, which emphasizes verbal knowledge and reasoning, is predominantly left-brain education. Guided fantasy offers the possibility of engaging the right half of the brain in the learning process. We know that experience is the best teacher and that teaching is easier when students have had relevant experiences. Some things, however, are difficult or impossible to experience directly. The use of fantasy, however, can give students an imaginary experience which they can relate to the verbal, logical material which is usually presented in class. In this way, material geared to left-brain learning can be connected to the more diffuse, intuitive knowing of the right side. Providing students with experiences to match the usual didactic instruction may also be a key to unlocking creative insight and intuitive understanding. Perhaps when something suddenly "makes sense" or "rings true," it is an instance of making a connection between the two modes of knowing. Becoming aware in the left side of the brain of what the right side had intuitively known but had not been able to verbalize may be experienced as a flash of insight.

Philosophers and psychologists of education, as well as teachers, curriculum planners, textbook writers, and material makers can learn from Ornstein's brain research that the linear, verbal-intellectual mode of knowing is clearly not the only mode available to man. What are other ways of teaching for other modes of learning? The field is open for reconceptualizing what it means to teach and to be educated, for creative classroom innovations, for research on new teaching styles, and for the development of new topics of study and supporting educational materials.

Learning to understand and control one's own consciousness includes learning to pay attention to what one wants when one wants to, instead of being at the mercy of a roaming, untrained mind. Learning how to relax, concentrate, and freely associate are skills which we seldom teach, but which give evidence of improving current instruction. They are also basic skills for developing further transpersonal potentials, in school, outside of school, and later in life. . . .

ALTERED STATES OF CONSCIOUSNESS

Western psychology has traditionally recognized only three states of consciousness, namely waking, dreaming, and dreamless sleep. Meditation, daydreaming, hypnosis, etc., have been considered variations of the waking state. In contrast, Buddhist psychology identifies well over a hundred different states of mind. Eastern psychologies apparently are more conceptually and theoretically sophisticated than Western psychologies in matters of subjective experience and altered states of consciousness.

The importance of altered states of consciousness for psychology was first recognized by William James, who stated:

Our normal waking consciousness, rational consciousness, as we call it, is but one special type of consciousness, whilst all about it, parted from it by the filmiest of screens, there lie potential forms of consciousness entirely different. No account of the universe in its totality can be final which leaves these other forms of consciousness quite discarded.

Some altered states are currently off limits for use in schools but may nevertheless be discussed. Hypnosis, for example, should be practiced only by a qualified hypnotherapist, but it is a fascinating topic for class discussion. Popular misconceptions regarding hypnosis can be cleared up easily in discussion with a well-informed teacher. Self-hypnosis deserves attention as a tool for accelerating learning as well as a method of gaining voluntary control over physiological functions.

Psychoactive drugs, including alcohol, coffee, and marijuana are on many students' minds. Andrew Weil, author of *The Natural Mind,* says people have an innate desire to alter consciousness. Forcing this topic underground, like forcing the topic of sex underground, results in misinformation, rumors, and unfortunate experiences. Open discussion of altered states of consciousness can throw some light on this mysterious topic and inform students that there are effective non-drug ways of exploring and controlling consciousness. A complete drug education program should recognize the natural human desire for exploring consciousness and should provide acceptable alternative routes.

Dreams

What is important for education is the fact that altered states of consciousness, particularly the dream state, are eagerly picked up by students at all levels of education as a topic of study. Dreaming is an altered state that is being used successfully by teachers both as technique and as content. From a transpersonal point of view, dreams are important because they give us messages from the unconscious, and they afford easy access to a different reality. Dreaming is one door to our inner selves. Furthermore, there is a considerable body of research on dreams, and dreaming is a state readily available to almost everyone.

Questions of how to interpret dreams will inevitably be a part of any classroom discussion. It is advisable for the teacher to point out that there are many different approaches to dream interpretation, and that each person can get more out of his dreams by exploring his own feelings and associations to the dream than out of a standard interpretation of symbols occurring in the dream. Interpretations often lead to blocking and forgetting of dreams, as well as being potentially destructive or misleading. When using dreams as a source of creativity or as a beginning of self-exploration, it is therefore advisable not to interpret the dreams, but to accept them as messages, or stories, one is telling oneself.

If some students have difficulty remembering dreams they can be reassured by a suggestion that if they do not remember one, they can make one up. Allowing a few minutes of quiet time before working with dreams can help the recall process and allow time for anybody who wants to make one up to do so. Initially, it is not important whether the dream is an actual dream or a made-up dream. Either way the student has a chance to explore and express his creative imagination.

Some methods which can help people remember dreams include lying quietly for a few minutes after waking up and reviewing dreams or dream fragments; setting an alarm in order to wake up at different times during the night to catch a dream in process; keeping a tape recorder or a paper and pencil next to the bed to record dreams immediately. Dreams which can be easily recalled immediately after waking may be forgotten in a short time, so it is a good idea to record them as soon as possible. Sharing dreams can often be a way of remembering more dreams, and listening to others may also remind a person of dreams he has forgotten. . . .

Keeping a dream diary can help even young children see recurring dreams and recurring themes from different dreams. Often the feeling that different dreams are related is a more reliable indicator of their relationship than reasoned comparison of their content. Asking students to retell their dreams in a dimmed classroom following relaxation helps the sharing process. One teacher completed her instructions this way: "After we have discussed one person's dreams and have given our own visualizations as well as emotions during that time, we will move to someone else. It is also important for you to know that you are invited to share your dreams which are, in effect, your inner life, only to the degree that you feel comfortable doing so."

The chairman of a high school English department used dreams this way:

I told them that I wanted them to be very quiet and try to crawl back inside their dream for about five minutes to "see" the way it was and to recapture the feeling the dream gave them. Then, they were to write just as fast as they could without worrying about literary style or mechanics. Their purpose was to get as much of their dream as possible down on paper in vivid, sharp, detailed language.

We turned out the lights and pulled the drapes. The room became semi-dark and very, very still.

I had expected some resistance or at least some embarrassed uneasiness; there was none. Some students leaned back and stretched their legs out in front of them; others put their heads on their desks; some just sat with their eyes closed. After about five minutes, one or two began to write. One by one in the next few minutes, they all began. No one broke the silence until a few seconds before the bell rang when I asked them to bring their papers (many of which were finished by this time) with them the next day.

At the beginning of the period the following day I asked them to go through what they had written and to select the most vital parts of their dream and the most vivid wording. Using what they selected, they were to write a poem. (We had only begun poetry, having spent two days of individual browsing/reading in poetry collections.) My only instructions to the students were that they should not try to use rhyme and they should "squeeze out" every excess word. . . .

The assignment, I felt, was a success for a number of reasons: 1. Everyone had something to write about. 2. The students were fascinated by dreams and uninhibited about sharing them. 3. The vivid quality of dreams lends itself to poetic expression.

It was, I think, the best first experience in poetry that I have ever tried.

Working with dreams carries the implicit message that the dream state is useful and worth studying. It gives students practice in using an altered state of consciousness and may encourage the exploration of other altered states which contain further resources that can be made available. An educational corollary to William James' statement is: No education of man can be complete which leaves these potential forms of consciousness undeveloped.

Meditation and Centering

Meditation has already received some coverage in educational journals. Studies of the transcendental type of meditation show improved self-control, improved social relations with fellow students, teachers, and parents, decreased drug abuse, improved grades, and increased self-actualization. The Illinois House of Representatives resolved, ". . . that all educational institutions, especially those under State of Illinois Jurisdiction, be strongly encouraged to study the feasibility of courses in Transcendental Meditation. . . ." Counselors trained in Zen meditation improved their scores on self-actualization and on empathy measurement scales. Meditation has also been found helpful to athletes and effective in other forms of physiological control. Hatha yoga, which has already been introduced in some departments of physical education, is one way of teaching mind/body relationships. Various kinds of meditation are forms of altered states of consciousness which have many different uses in education. . . .

Centering exercises provide a good introduction to meditation, and are also helpful in quieting down. The process of centering can begin by focusing attention on the physical center of gravity in the body, feeling the relationship of the body to the earth and the space surrounding it. Experiencing the sense of balance and support provided by the floor or the chair helps to focus attention on physical sensations. Attention may be directed to the surface of the skin, body boundaries, and the flow of energy associated with the circulatory system. In many Eastern traditions, including the Japanese martial arts, the center of physical energy is located in the belly, about two inches below the navel, and two inches in front of the spine. Focusing attention on this center while noticing the movements of breathing in and out is an easy and widely used method of centering. Centering has a calming effect which makes concentration easier and helps students let go of distracting anxieties by focusing on being here and now. A good question to ask after giving instructions for relaxation or centering is "How does it feel to be you at this moment?" Do not expect a verbal answer. Allowing an experience of feeling without having to explain or name it is an important step in learning about oneself.

Another way of introducing meditation in a classroom is simply to suggest that students spend five minutes sitting in silence, with eyes closed. Additional instructions may be given, such as counting breaths from one to ten, and then starting at number one again, or visualizing a symbol such as a circle, cross, or triangle. Such additional instructions may make it easier for beginners to remain quiet and still, but are not essential. The instructions may be equally effective when students are asked to just sit. As the practice becomes more familiar, the period of time can be increased to twenty or thirty minutes, depending on the circumstances. Images which often emerge spontaneously during a period of meditation may also be a source of subject matter for discussion. Such imagery may be treated in the same way as dreams. A popular form of meditation among those who have not tried it before is observation meditation, where the students are instructed to simply observe themselves, and whatever is present on the physical (sensations), emotional (feelings), and mental (thoughts) levels. This process often facilitates awareness of inner imagery. . . .

Biofeedback

Biofeedback has been widely reported in the professional and popular press, and there is little need to go into detail here except as it applies to transpersonal educational interests. By amplifying activities inside the human body so that we can listen to internal processes such as heartbeat, blood pressure, brain activity, skin resistance, and many more, much of the autonomic nervous system can be brought under voluntary control. These previously hidden abilities of self-control open up whole new ranges for teaching physical education, health, and/or biology.

After seeing the film *Involuntary Control* at Sycamore High School in rural Illinois, some of the students tried some inexpensive biofeedback equipment borrowed from Northern Illinois University. One adolescent boy showed remarkable ability to raise and lower his galvanic skin response, a measure of general emotional excitability. "You can sure tell the girls I like," he said, as he looked from one to another around the room. By listening to the tone of the machine and by correlating it with his internal feelings, he was able to combine awareness of his own feelings with biofeedback knowledge from the galvanic skin response machine. If physical education means learning to control our bodies for optimum health and physical fitness, biofeedback has an important place coming in the curriculum of the late 1970s.

If every young student *knew* by the time he finished his first biology class, in grade school, that the body responds to self-generated psychological inputs, that blood flow and heart behavior, as well as a host of other body processes, can be influenced at will, it would change prevailing ideas about both physical and mental health. It would then be quite clear and understandable that we are individually responsible to a large extent for our state of health or disease. Perhaps then people would begin to realize that it is not life that kills us, but rather it is our reaction to it, and this reaction can be to a significant extent self-chosen. (E. Green, A. Green, D. Walters, "Biofeedback for Mind-Body Self-Regulation: Healing and Creativity." Menninger Foundation)

Biofeedback training also provides an interesting link between transpersonal psychology and behavioral psychology. The way a person learns to control these previously automatic functions is simply by being rewarded for doing the right thing to achieve his purpose, whether it be to cure a migraine headache, slow down his heart, or increase blood flow to injured organs. Even though he usually cannot explain what he is doing or how he is doing it, the feedback that he is accomplishing it is enough reward to improve his performance.

An even more exciting link is being explored between the biofeedback conditioning of brain waves and parapsychology. The biochemical activities of the brain produce electrical current that pulses at different speeds:

delta	0–4 times a second
theta	5–7 times a second
alpha	8–14 times a second
beta	15–30 times a second

Different frequencies predominate as a person goes into different kinds of awareness. For adults, beta is the normal waking state; alpha is a relaxed state bordering sleep; theta is associated with dreams; and delta is very deep sleep or coma. These frequencies are also associated with various altered states of consciousness. Some provocative research conducted by the Greens at the Menninger Foundation, and by Stanley Krippner and Montague Ullman at Maimonides Hospital in Brooklyn, indicates that both creativity and telepathy may be enhanced by alpha and theta conditioning. Yogic Masters develop complicated and precise control of their physiology, including brain waves. Could this partially account for the paranormal power attributed to advanced yogis? Could this physiological control also account for some instances of psychic healing?

Parapsychology

Parapsychological topics make excellent class reports. Students enjoy learning about parapsychology and doing their own experiments. The readings may be newspaper articles, inexpensive paperbacks, or highly statistical journal articles. Subjects which were formerly taboo for "respectable" psychologists are opening up, and they provide an excellent example of how fields of knowledge change with the times. One of the hardest ideas to get across to students is that things are not always true or false. With scientific controversy surrounding parapsychology, it provides a natural topic for teaching how science expands to include new observations and how our ideas of acceptability adjust from time to time. Since many people see parapsychology in the gray area between belief and disbelief, a good teacher can capitalize on this to teach students that it is perfectly respectable intellectually to be undecided about conflicting information and that knowledge progresses by exploring these gray areas. One way to teach about parapsychology and other transpersonal topics is to treat them similarly to the way the theory of evolution was taught earlier in this century. They can be presented as ideas which some people believe and others don't, without necessarily having been proven true or false. A teacher can simply say, "Here is what some psychologists are saying . . . and here is the reasoning that disbelievers use. . . ." The confrontation is taking place between people who cite empirical evidence and want to change ways of thinking, and those who side with accepted ways of thinking and criticize the evidence: a classic battle between observation and reason.

Parapsychology is the scientific study of facts which do not fit in with the established theories of man which assume that he knows the world only through his senses. Selections from books such as *Psychic Discoveries Behind the Iron Curtain, ESP: A Curriculum Guide,* and *Dream Telepathy* can guide teachers. Investigation into parapsychology leads into other transpersonal areas too, as parapsychology is often linked with dreaming, relaxed receptivity, and other altered states. For example, states of consciousness associated with the alpha and theta brain-wave patterns are frequently associated with parapsychological events in which ordinary limitations of time and space are apparently transcended. Movies on parapsychology are also informative and provocative, and are primarily oriented toward high school and college audiences.

Stanley Krippner, president of the Association for Humanistic Psychology, and Gardner Murphy, past-president of the American Psychological Association, suggest links between successful teaching and student-teacher ESP. There is also some evidence that parapsychological abilities are not just "gifts" or inherent traits, but that they can be learned.

Spirituality

Investigation of the phenomena of transcendence and peak experiences has also reawakened interest in spiritual experiences associated with higher states of consciousness, sometimes called cosmic consciousness, mystical union, or enlightenment. Barry McWaters has indicated:

Within the past five years there has been a resurgence of both personal and empirical exploration of altered states of consciousness in which the individual experiences himself as having transcended the limitations of his ordinary waking consciousness. Physical phenomena, such as clairvoyance and astral projection, and religious phenomena, such as speaking in tongues and mystical union, are examples of transpersonal experiences. (Barry McWaters, "An Outline of Transpersonal Psychology: Its Meaning and Relevance for Education")

Some transpersonal psychologists are attempting a systematic study of spiritual experiences. Mystics, psychics, physicists, and other scientists often report their perceptions of the universe in almost identical terms. Furthermore, if adjustments are made to account for cultural differences, mystics from all over the world agree on the phenomenology of mystic experiences. Research on psychic healers at the Menninger Foundation indicates that some healers describe a "field of mind" that surrounds the earth just as the magnetic, radiation, and gravitational fields surround it. Healers seem to be able to tune in to this force, suggesting the possibility that other people can learn to do this, perhaps through biofeedback training or developing other self-controlled altered states of consciousness.

Interest in man's spiritual aspirations forms one of the historical and conceptual links between transpersonal psychology and humanistic psychology.* A.H. Maslow, one of the founders of humanistic psychology, proposed a five-stage theory of human motivation. In his studies of self-actualizers he discovered that this group reported peak experiences more frequently than other groups. Following this lead brought him to the study of transcendent experiences. In some of his later work he describes two kinds of self-actualizers, and seemed on the verge of adding a sixth stage of motivation: self-transcendence, or a motivation for cosmic consciousness. Humanistic psychologists have used the first five stages in counseling, teaching, and planning curricula. Perhaps a sixth, transcendent, stage would be helpful in considering student motivation.

Assuming such motivation helps explain why students like certain kinds of drug highs, and it simultaneously suggests that schools can help reduce drug abuse by teaching alternate means of achieving higher states of consciousness. Peak experiences and altered states occurring in poetry and prose are readily available for exploration. They are useful concepts in the literature of self-actualization and can serve as a focus for developing language skills. In social studies or other classes which consider why people do things, the desire for spiritual or transcendent experiences

---

*The transpersonal psychology movement was initiated largely by humanistic psychologists who wanted to expand beyond the humanistic movement's primary concern with interpersonal interaction. Transpersonal psychologists and educators, while recognizing the importance of interpersonal dynamics, tend to focus more on intrapersonal and transpersonal experience, the latter being that inner set which all persons share.—Ed.

helps explain human behavior. For example, much religious and cultural conflict stems from disagreement over what mystical experiences are and who has the best way of achieving them, leading to religious wars, persecution, and other intercultural conflicts. The interpretation of transcendent experiences is central to the religions and world views of different cultures. Transpersonal psychology is useful in its acceptance and study of transcendent, or spiritual, experiences as an important aspect of human nature and a legitimate field for psychological investigation. The scientific interest in transcendent experiences should not be confused with teaching religion. From a psychological standpoint, experiences are considered empirically, without resorting to metaphysical interpretation or dogmatic assumptions. As in working with dreams and fantasy, interpretations are likely to inhibit sharing of experience, and a student's subjective interpretation of his own experience should be respected.

Growth Potential

After visiting a growth center and reading some articles on transpersonal psychology, an eighth-grade teacher developed a unit called "Growth Potential." The main theme was that all human beings have vast potentials that are seldom used. He included unusual cases of physical prowess and athletic records, new inventions and medicines, suggestibility, parapsychology, fantasy, and other neglected human skills. "Everyone seemed to enjoy the experience," he reported. "The only problem for me was the insistence on doing it again. Imagination, creativity, frank and open discussion were all results of what we had tried."

Teachers are often surprised at how eagerly students respond to transpersonal teaching techniques. Some of these approaches seem to awaken the natural desire in each of us to explore our inner selves:

I have been overwhelmed by the willingness and ability of the children to remain completely still, without a motion, for 30 minutes. Six months ago I would have laughed at the idea. Julio Sanchez, an extremely active child, seems calmed down considerably. He also gets down to work much more quickly. . . . We talked about the directed dreams of Malayan children and the different ways in which dreams could better be remembered or evoked. During all of our talks the class (6th grade) was in a state which only elementary teachers really understand. All eyes on whoever the speaker was, no outside interruptions, mouths open. Once started it was amazing how eagerly children want to look inward and learn about themselves.

The teacher's experience is typical. The first time an unusual teaching technique is tried, there may be some resistance or silliness, but it almost always disappears the second time. Is this because we all have a natural desire to explore inner potentials? Perhaps dreams are successful as content because it is content that each person experiences, not just learning about something "out there," that seems to have no personal relevance.

Further development of classroom exercises is possible in the adaptation of adult-oriented exercises to schools, with a focus on developing skills which would enable students to continue personal and transpersonal growth on their own time or after they graduate. Such books as *Mind Games, Awareness,* and *Passages* provide adult learning exercises. Educators can use these to continue their own growth and as sources for classroom adaptions. Under a grant from the Quebec Ministry of Education, the Canadian Institute of Psychosynthesis has developed classroom techniques for humanistic and transpersonal growth. In the United States, psychosynthesis groups in New York City and Redwood City, California, are adapting other growth techniques developed by Roberto Assagioli to the classroom and to counseling.

FUTURE TRENDS AND IMPLICATIONS

Research

Research in transpersonal educational psychology is currently at the exploratory and descriptive stages. However, some rough-hewn applications of transpersonal ideas show considerable promise. Whenever new practices come along, the door is open to common research, which compares and evaluates new methods. Descriptive and exploratory research by teachers indicates increased content learned, student enthusiasm, student self-control, excitement in self-exploration, and investigation of topics usually shunted to the side in traditional as well as innovative schools. Relaxation, focusing, meditation, and other transpersonal practices are open fields for traditional educational research.

The importance of subjective empiricism as a method of investigation should not be overlooked, nor should the experimenter imagine himself neutral during research.

A discipline comes of age and a student of that discipline reaches maturity when it becomes possible to recognize, estimate, and allow for the errors of their tools. . . . Yet there is one instrument which every discipline uses without checking its errors, tacitly assuming that the instrument is error-free. This, of course, is the human psychological apparatus. As a result of the failure to consider the sources of error in the human being himself, when our academic disciplines assemble together in our great educational institutions, they re-enforce the tacit, fallacious assumption that man can understand the world that lies outside of himself without concurrently understanding himself. Actually, each man is his own microscope with his own idiosyncracies, to which he alone can penetrate. (Lawrence S. Kubie, "The Forgotten Man of Education")

Considering the state of consciousness as a major variable of all behavior is filled with implications. This is a previously disregarded variable in every experiment and during all teaching. If we erroneously assume there is only one state of consciousness or that all awake people are in the same state, we are neglecting this important variable. Various states of consciousness, their intensities or optimal combinations, may be a major set of variables for a new generation of educational researchers to study. Instead of changing the external stimuli given to a student, can we effect greater changes by teaching him to control his own state of consciousness?

Perhaps relaxation, receptivity, focusing, concentration, holistic perception, linear perception, reasoning, analysis, brain-wave patterns, and left-brain and right-brain activity are some of the basic mental variables. Just as reading and arithmetic are foundation skills for the intellectual, left-brain activities, there may also be primary-level skills such as fantasy, dreaming, concentration, and other skills that will allow us to develop and use the intuitive, right sides of our brains.

Teacher Education

During inservice education, teachers frequently go through three stages when they are introduced to transpersonal psychology. At first they are puzzled, put off, or simply confused. Since a transpersonal approach to education required them to look at their work in a different light, this is not surprising. The next step is accepting one or two ideas for applying a transpersonal technique in their classrooms, or introducing some transpersonal content into their lessons. This is usually dreams, some form of ESP such as a classroom experiment, discussion of psychic phenomena, or a combination of relaxation and fantasy.

Finally, having tried a transpersonal innovation, they are enthusiastic and eager to do more. I have found undergraduates generally more willing to accept transpersonal content such as ESP, psychic phenomena, and altered states of consciousness, while inservice teachers are more willing to believe that developing right-brain potentials is worth doing and that it can be done.

Here is a new realm for teacher education. Along with the cognitive, affective, and psychomotor domains, we now have the transpersonal domain. Each subject area has its transpersonal content tool. Work needs to be done on a basic information level for teachers, objective writers, textbook publishers, testing services, and others in the educational support services who prepare materials. Much of the original transpersonal research needs to be rewritten so that school students can understand it. Some existing materials can be enlarged, while entirely new lines of transpersonal materials remain to be created.

How do we prepare teachers for their roles as transpersonal educators? A new kind of teacher education and a new breed of teacher-educators are needed too. Here is a wide-open opportunity for colleges of education. If we look back at the rise and fall of educational psychologies and the rise and fall of various colleges of education, we see that frequently certain schools staked out a new educational psychology and built much of their reputation on developing it. A good part of the reputation of Teacher's College at Columbia Unversity was due to faculty members who were influential in the application of Freudian psychology to education. Stanford, Kansas, and other universities are making themselves well known in teacher education by applying behaviorism to education. Humanistic psychology applied to education is important at the colleges of education at the University of Massachusetts and at the University of California at Santa Barbara. While several institutions of higher education are flirting with transpersonal educational psychology, none has yet staked a claim and consciously built a reputation for transpersonal teacher education. Here too, there are more tantalizing possibilities than tested programs.

Philosophy

Our focus here has been primarily on those applications of transpersonal psychology which can be adapted to education immediately. However, the underlying philosophical assumptions have implications which go far beyond new teaching techniques, and which present new problems for educational philosophers to work on.

A transpersonal approach involves new, open concepts which are still being developed and clarified. For example, the concept of *consciousness* carries a new meaning in this context. It has expanded to include many different subjective and physiological states of consciousness, and should not be confused with terms such as political consciousness or social consiousness. Currently there is considerable interest in theoretically conceptualizing, or "mapping," inner states, in exploring methods for altering consciousness, and in evaluating the importance of altered states.

The mind/body problem is central to transpersonal education. It is clear that mental and emotional states affect the body, and that physical states affect the mind and emotions. The implication here is that the relationship between body and mind is far more complex and important than was previously believed. Transpersonal psychology is concerned with the integration of physical, emotional, mental, and spiritual development. It also assumes that man as a living organism is continually evolving, and capable of developing many capacities which have hitherto been neglected. Since we are concerned with the growing edge of human development, we are continually expanding the range of topics and finding new ways of learning. The meaning of the word "knowledge" itself is changing and expanding. Knowledge is no longer limited to objective subject matter or content. Awareness of inner states, experimental learning, ESP, and control of various autonomic functions are forms of knowledge which are not being incorporated in education. Since inner states cannot be observed by anyone other than the experiencing subject, subjective empiricism has become an important method of investigation.

New cross-cultural values are also emerging. The study of peak experiences and human potentials has led to a new appreciation of Eastern philosophies, and new definitions of "the good." As communication with other cultures has expanded, we now have the opportunity to learn more about alternate methods of training the mind and body. Interestingly, contemporary physicists are now describing reality in terms which coincide with the traditional views of mystics from many different religious traditions. This view affirms the essential unity of all life. This basic unity of man with his fellow men, with the environment, and with the cosmos is also affirmed in parapsychology, and is an underlying assumption in psychic healing and other psychic phenomena such as clairvoyance and telepathy. Researchers at the Menninger Foundation are investigating the speculation that there is a "field of mind" similar to the earth's magnetic field. Thoughts and ideas may exist in this field, and some people may even be able to tune in to it.

The emerging philosophy of education based on transpersonal psychology may be described as a combination of rational-analytic and intuitive-synthetic modes of knowing. With its origins in analytic philosophy, much educational thought has mistakenly equated "thinking" with "reasoning." Rational thinking, associated with the left hemisphere of the brain, is characteristically verbal, logical, analytic, and linear. Intuitive thinking, associated with the right hemisphere, is creative, holistic, visual, and pattern-oriented. Its strength is in seeing similarities, patterns, and agreements among ideas rather than analyzing differences and conflicts. Intuitive perception frequently appears to transcend or anticipate reason. Philosophies of education which do not recognize the importance of developing right-brain hemisphere potentials are seriously underestimating the human capacity for learning.

A man, having looted a city, was trying to sell an exquisite rug, one of the spoils. "Who will give 100 pieces of gold for this rug?" he cried throughout the town.

After the sale was completed, a comrade approached the seller and asked, "Why did you not ask more for that priceless rug?" "Is there any number higher than 100?" asked the seller. (Folk Tale from Central Asia, quoted from *The Psychology of Consciousness,* Robert Ornstein)

A newly opened image of man assumes that we are capable of knowing, being, and doing far more than we thought possible even a decade ago. As we continue to learn more about transpersonal dimensions of human experience, our vision of the future and the development of human potentials is constantly expanding. It is important to recognize the necessity for educating the whole person if we are to improve the human condition. Explorations in the study of consciousness hold considerable promise for education in the future.

From *Island*

Aldous Huxley

Aldous Huxley was the author of dozens of fiction and nonfiction books. Many of his works explore the farther reaches of the human potential.

The main character of Island, *Will Farnaby, is a journalist who comes to the utopian island with cynicism and doubt, but gradually sees the new heights in human potential being reached there. In this selection we are introduced to the island's educational system through a conversation between Will and Mr. Menon, the Under-Secretary of Education.*

"And the way to the Way of Disinterested Action is what I was looking at yesterday," said Will. "The way that leads through woodchopping and rock climbing—is that it?"

"Wood chopping and rock climbing," said Mr. Menon, "are special cases. Let's generalize and say that the way to *all* the Ways leads through the redirection of power."

"What's that?"

From *Island* by Aldous Huxley (New York: Harper & Row, 1962), pp. 212–32. Reprinted by permission of Mrs. Laura Huxley, Harper & Row, Publishers, Inc., and Chatto and Windus Ltd.

"The principle is very simple. You take the power generated by fear or envy or too much noradrenalin, or else by some built-in urge that happens, at the moment, to be out of place—you take it and, instead of using it to do something unpleasant to someone else, instead of repressing it and so doing something unpleasant to yourself, you consciously direct it along a channel where it can do something useful, or, if not useful, at least harmless."

"Here's a simple case," said the Principal. "An angry or frustrated child has worked up enough power for a burst of crying, or bad language, or a fight. If the power generated is sufficient for any of those things, it's significant for running, or dancing, more than sufficient for five deep breaths. I'll show you some dancing later on. For the moment, let's confine ourselves to breathing. Any irritated person who takes five deep breaths releases a lot of tension and so makes it easier for himself to behave rationally. So we teach our children all kinds of breathing games, to be played whenever they're angry or upset. Some of the games are competitive. Which of two antagonists can inhale most deeply and say 'om' on the outgoing breath for the longest time? It's a duel that ends, almost without fail, in reconciliation. But of course there are many occasions when competitive breathing is out of place. So here's a little game that an exasperated child can play on his own, a game that's based on the local folklore. Every Palanese child has been brought up on Buddhist legends, and in most of these pious fairy stories somebody has a vision of a celestial being. A Bodhisattva, say, in an explosion of lights, jewels and rainbows. And along with the glorious vision there's always an equally glorious olfaction; the fireworks are accompanied by an unutterably delicious perfume. Well, we take these traditional phantasies —which are all based, needless to say, on actual visionary experiences of the kind induced by fasting, sensory deprivation or mushrooms—and we set them to work. Violent feelings, we tell the children, are like earthquakes. They shake us so hard that cracks appear in the wall that separates our private selves from the shared, universal Buddha Nature. You get cross, something inside of you cracks and, through the crack, out comes a whiff of the heavenly smell of enlightenment. Like champak, like ylang-ylang, like gardenias—only infinitely more wonderful. So don't miss this heavenliness that you've accidentally released. It's there every time you get cross. Inhale it, breathe it in, fill your lungs with it. Again and again."

"And they actually do it?"

"After a few weeks of teaching, most of them do it as a matter of course. And, what's more, a lot of them really smell that perfume. The old repressive 'Thou shalt not' has been translated into a new expressive and rewarding 'Thou shalt.' Potentially harmful power has been redirected into channels where it's not merely harmless, but may actually do some good. And meanwhile, of course, we've been giving the children systematic and carefully graduated training in perception and the proper use of language. They're taught to pay attention to what they see and hear, and at the same time they're asked to notice how their feelings and desires affect what they experience of the outer world, and how their language habits affect not only their feelings and desires but even their sensations. What my ears and my eyes record is one thing; what the words I use and the mood I'm in and the purposes I'm pursuing allow me to perceive, make sense of and act upon is something quite different. So you see it's all brought together into a single educational process. What we give the children is simultaneously a training in perceiving and imagining, a training in applied physiology and psychology, a training in practical ethics and practical religion, a training in the proper use of language, and a training in self-knowledge. In a word, a training of the whole mind-body in all its aspects."

"What's the relevance," Will asked, "of all this elaborate training of the mind-body to formal education? Does it help a child to do sums, or write grammatically, or understand elementary physics?"

"It helps a lot," said Mr. Menon. "A trained mind-body learns more quickly and more thoroughly than an untrained one. It's also more capable of relating facts to ideas, and both of them to its own ongoing life." Suddenly and surprisingly—for that long melancholy face gave one the impression of being incompatible with any expression of mirth more emphatic than a rather weary smile—he broke into a loud long peal of laughter.

"What's the joke?"

"I was thinking of two people I met last time I was in England. At Cambridge. One of them was an atomic physicist, the other was a philosopher. Both extremely eminent. But one had a mental age, outside the laboratory, of about eleven and the other was a compulsive eater with a weight problem that he refused to face. Two extreme examples of what happens when you take a clever boy, give him fifteen years of the most intensive formal education and totally neglect to do anything for the mind-body which has to do the learning and the living."

"And your system, I take it, doesn't produce that kind of academic monster?"

The Under-Secretary shook his head. "Until I went to Europe, I'd never seen anything of the kind. They're grotesquely funny," he added. "But, goodness, how pathetic. And, poor things, how curiously repulsive!"

"Being pathetically and curiously repulsive—that's the price we pay for specilization."

"For specialization," Mr. Menon agreed, "but not in the sense you people ordinarily use the word. Specialization in that sense is necessary and inevitable. No specialization, no civilization. And if one educates the whole mind-body along with the symbol-using intellect, that kind of necessary specialization won't do much harm. But you people don't educate the mind-body. Your cure for too much scientific specialization is a few more courses in the humanities. Excellent! Every education ought to include courses in the humanities. But don't let's be fooled by the name. By themselves, the humanities don't humanize. They're simply another form of specialization on the symbolic level. Reading Plato or listening to a lecture on T.S. Eliot doesn't educate the whole human being; like courses in physics or chemistry, it merely educates the symbol manipulator and leaves the rest of the living mind-body in its pristine state of ignorance and ineptitude. Hence all those pathetic and repulsive creatures that so astonished me on my first trip abroad."

"What about formal education?" Will now asked. "What about indispensable information and the necessary intellectual skills? Do you teach the way we do?"

"We teach the way you're probably going to teach in another ten or fifteen years. Take mathematics, for example. Historically mathematics began with the elaboration of useful tricks, soared up into metaphysics and finally explained itself in terms of structure and logical transformations. In our schools we reverse the historical process. We begin with structure and logic; then, skipping the metaphysics, we go on from general principles to particular applications."

"And the children understand?"

"Far better than they understand when one starts with utilitarian tricks. From about five onwards practically any intelligent child can learn practically anything, provided always that you present it to him in the right way. Logic and structure in the form of games and puzzles. The children play and, incredibly quickly, they catch the point. After which you can go on to practical applications. Taught in this way, most children can learn at least three times as much, four times as thoroughly, in half the time. Or consider another field where one can use games to implant an understanding of basic principles. All scientific thinking is in terms of probability. The old eternal verities are merely a high degree of likeliness; the immutable laws of nature are just statistical averages. How does one get these profoundly unobvious notions into children's heads? By playing roulette with them, by spinning coins and drawing lots. By teaching them all kinds of games with cards and boards and dice.''

"Evolutionary Snakes and Ladders—that's the most popular game with the little ones," said Mrs. Narayan. "Another great favorite is Mendelian Happy Families.''

"And a little later," Mr. Menon added, "we introduce them to a rather complicated game played by four people with a pack of sixty specially designed cards divided into three suits. Psychological bridge, we call it. Chance deals you your hand, but the way you play it is a matter of skill, bluff and co-operation with your partner.''

"Psychology, Mendelism, Evolution—your education seems to be heavily biological," said Will.

"It *is,*" Mr. Menon agreed. "Our primary emphasis isn't on physics and chemistry; it's on the sciences of life.''

"Is that a matter of principle?'' . . .

"Mathematics," said the Principal as she opened a door. "And this is the Upper Fifth. Under Mrs. Anand.''

Will bowed as he was introduced. The white-haired teacher gave a welcoming smile and whispered, "We're deep, as you see, in a problem.''

He looked about him. At their desks a score of boys and girls were frowning, in a concentrated, pencil-biting silence, over their notebooks. The bent heads were sleek and dark. Above the white or khaki shorts, above the long gaily colored skirts, the golden bodies glistened in the heat. Boys' bodies that showed the cage of the ribs beneath the skin, girls' bodies, fuller, smoother, with the swell of small breasts, firm, high-set, elegant as the inventions of a rococo sculptor of nymphs. And everyone took them completely for granted. What a comfort, Will reflected, to be in a place where the Fall was an exploded doctrine!

Meanwhile, Mrs. Anand was explaining—*sotto voce* so as not to distract the problem solvers from their task—that she always divided her classes into two groups. The group of the visualizers, who thought in geometrical terms, like the ancient Greeks, and the group of the nonvisualizers who preferred algebra and imageless abstractions. Somewhat reluctantly Will withdrew his attention from the beautiful unfallen world of young bodies and resigned himself to taking an intelligent interest in human diversity and the teaching of mathematics.

They took their leave at last. Next door, in a pale-blue classroom decorated with paintings of tropical animals, Bodhisattvas and their bosomy Shaktis, the Lower Fifth were having their biweekly lesson in Elementary Applied Philosophy. Breasts here were smaller, arms thinner and less muscular. These philosophers were only a year away from childhood.

"Symbols are public," the young man at the blackboard was saying as Will and Mrs. Narayan entered the room. He drew a row of little circles, numbered them 1, 2, 3, 4, and *n*. "These are people," he explained. Then from each of the little circles he drew a line that connected it with a square at the left of the board. S he wrote in the center of the square. "S is the system of symbols that the people use when they want to talk to one another. They all speak the same language—English, Palanese, Eskimo, it depends where they happen to live. Words are public; they belong to all the speakers of a given language; they're listed in dictionaries. And now let's look at the things that happen out there." He pointed through the open window. Gaudy against a white cloud, half a dozen parrots came sailing into view, passed behind a tree and were gone. The teacher drew a second square at the opposite side of the board, labeled it E for "events" and connected it by lines to the circles. "What happens out there is public —or at least fairly public," he qualified. "And what happens when somebody speaks or writes words—that's also public. But the things that go on inside these little circles are private. Private." He laid a hand on his chest. "Private." He rubbed his forehead. "Private." He touched his eyelids and the tip of his nose with a brown forefinger. "Now let's make a simple experiment. Say the word 'pinch.' "

"Pinch," said the class in ragged unison, "Pinch . . ."

"P-I-N-C-H—pinch. That's public, that's something you can look up in the dictionary. But now pinch yourselves. Hard! Harder!"

To an accompaniment of giggles, of *aies* and *ows*, the children did as they were told.

"Can anybody feel what the person sitting next to him is feeling?"

There was a chorus of noes.

"So it looks," said the young man, "as though there were—let's see, how many are we?" He ran his eyes over the desks before him. "It looks as though there were twenty-three distinct and separate pains. Twenty-three in this one room. Nearly three thousand million of them in the whole world. Plus the pains of all the animals. And each of these pains from one center of pain to another center of pain. No communication except indirectly through S." He pointed to the square at the left of the board, then to the circles at the center. "Private pains here in 1, 2, 3, 4, and *n*. News about private pains out here at S, where you can say 'pinch,' which is a public word listed in a dictionary. And notice this: there's only one public word, 'pain,' for three thousand million private experiences, each of which is probably about as different from all the others as my nose is different from your noses and your noses are different from one another. A word only stands for the ways in which things or happenings of the same general kind are like one another. That's why the word is public. And, being public, it can't possibly stand for the ways in which happenings of the same general kind are unlike one another."

There was a silence. Then the teacher looked up and asked a question.

"Does anyone here know about Mahakasyapa?"

Several hands were raised. He pointed his finger at a little girl in a blue skirt and a necklace of shells sitting in the front row.

"You tell us, Amiya."

Breathlessly and with a lisp, Amiya began.

"Mahakathyapa," she said, "wath the only one of the dithipleth that underthtood what the Buddha wath talking about."

"And what was he talking about?"

"He wathn't talking. That'th why they didn't underthand."

"But Mahakasyapa understood what he was talking about even though he wasn't talking—is that it?"

The little girl nodded. That was it exactly. "They thought he wath going to preath a thermon," she said, "but he didn't. He jutht picked a flower and held it up for everybody to look at."

"And that was the sermon," shouted a small boy in a yellow loincloth, who had been wriggling in his seat, hardly able to contain his desire to impart what he knew. "But nobody could underthand that kind of a thermon. Nobody but Mahakathyapa."

"So what did Mahakasyapa say when the Buddha held up that flower?"

"Nothing!" the yellow loincloth shouted triumphantly.

"He jutht thmiled," Amiya elaborated. "And that thowed the Buddha that he underthtood what it wath all about. So he thmiled back, and they jutht that there, thmiling and thmiling."

"Very good," sid the teacher. "And now," he turned to the yellow loincloth, "let's hear what you think it was that Mahakasyapa understood."

There was a silence. Then, crestfallen, the child shook his head. "I don't know," he mumbled.

"Does anyone else know?"

There were several conjectures. Perhaps he'd understood that people get bored with sermons—even the Buddha's sermons. Perhaps he liked flowers as much as the Compassionate One did. Perhaps it was a white flower, and that made him think of the Clear Light. Or perhaps it was blue, and that was Shiva's color.

"Good answers," said the teacher. "Especially the first one. Sermons *are* pretty boring—especially for the preacher. But here's a question. If any of your answers had been what Mahakasyapa understood when Buddha held up the flower, why didn't he come out with it in so many words?"

"Perhaps he wathn't a good thpeaker."

"He was an excellent speaker."

"Maybe he had a sore throat."

"If he'd had a sore throat, he wouldn't have smiled so happily."

"*You* tell us," called a shrill voice from the back of the room.

"Yes, *you* tell us," a dozen other voices chimed in.

The teacher shook his head. "If Mahakasyapa and the Compassionate One couldn't put it into words, how can I? Meanwhile let's take another look at these diagrams on the blackboard. Public words, more or less public events, and then people, completely private centers of pain and pleasure. "*Completely* private?" he questioned. "But perhaps that isn't quite true. Perhaps, after all, there is some kind of communication between the circles—not in the way I'm communicating with you now; through words, but directly. And maybe that was what the Buddha was talking about when his wordless flower-sermon was over. 'I have the treasure of the unmistakable teachings,' he said to his disciples, 'the wonderful Mind of Nirvana, the true form without form, beyond all words, the teaching to be given and received outside of all doctrines. This I have now handed to Mahakasyapa.' " Picking up the chalk again, he traced a rough ellipse that enclosed within its boundaries all the other diagrams on the board—the little circles representing human beings, the square that stood for events, and the other square that stood for words and symbols. "All separate," he said, "and yet all one. People, events, words—they're all manifestations of Mind, of Suchness, of the Void.

What Buddha was implying and what Mahakasyapa understood was that one can't speak these teachings, one can only *be* them. Which is something you'll all discover when the moment comes for your initiation.''

"Time to move on," the Principal whispered. And when the door had closed behind them, and they were standing again in the corridor, "We use this same kind of approach," she said to Will, "in our science teaching, beginning with botany."

"Why with botany?"

"Because it can be related so easily to what was being talked about just now—the Mahakasyapa story."

"Is that your starting point?"

"No, we start prosaically with the textbook. The children are given all the obvious, elementary facts, tidily arranged in the standard pigeon-holes. Undiluted botany—that's the first stage. Six or seven weeks of it. After which they get a whole morning of what we call bridge building. Two and a half hours during which we try to make them relate everything they've learned in the previous lessons to art, language, religion, self-knowledge."

"Botany and self-knowledge—how do you build *that* bridge?"

"It's really quite simple," Mrs. Narayan assured him. "Each of the children is given a common flower—a hibiscus, for example, or better still (because the hibiscus has no scent) a gardenia. Scientifically speaking, what is a gardenia? What does it consist of? Petals, stamens, pistil, ovary, and all the rest of it. The children are asked to write a full analytical description of the flower, illustrated by an accurate drawing. When that's done there's a short rest period, at the close of which the Mahakasyapa story is read to them and they're asked to think about it. Was Buddha giving a lesson in botany? Or was he teaching his disciples something else? And, if so, what?"

"What indeed?"

"And of course, as the story makes clear, there's no answer that can be put into words. So we tell the boys and girls to stop thinking and just look. 'But don't look analytically,' we tell them, 'don't look as scientists, even as gardeners. Liberate yourselves from everything you know and look with complete innocence at this infinitely improbable thing before you. Look at it as though you'd never seen anything of the kind before, as though it had no name and belonged to no recognizable class. Look at it alertly but passively, receptively, without labeling or judging or comparing. And as you look at it, inhale its mystery, breathe in the spirit of sense, the smell of the wisdom of the Other Shore.' "

"All this," Will commented, "sounds very like what Dr. Robert was saying at the initiation ceremony."

"Of course it does," said Mrs. Narayan. "Learning to take the Mahakasyapa's-eye view of things is the best preparation for the *moksha*-medicine experience. Every child who comes to initiation comes to it after a long education in the art of being receptive. First the gardenia as a botanical specimen. Then the same gardenia in its uniqueness, the gardenia as the artist sees it, the even more miraculous gardenia seen by the Buddha and Mahakasyapa. And it goes without saying," she added, "that we don't confine ourselves to flowers. Every course the children take is punctuated by periodical bridge-building sessions. Everything from dissected frogs to the spiral nebulae, it all gets looked at receptively as well as conceptually, as a fact of aesthetic or spiritual experience as well as in terms of science or history or economics. Training in receptivity is the complement and antidote to training in analysis and symbol manipulation. Both kinds of training are absolutely indispensable. If you neglect either of them you'll never grow into a fully human being."

. . .

They crossed a tree-shaded courtyard and, pushing through a swing door, passed out of silence into the rhythmic beat of a drum and the screech of fifes repeating over and over again a short pentatonic tune that to Will's ears sounded vaguely Scotch.

"Live music or canned?" he asked.

"Japanese tape," Mrs. Narayan answered laconically. She opened a second door that gave access to a large gymnasium where two bearded young men and an amazingly agile little old lady in black satin slacks were teaching some twenty to thirty little boys and girls the steps of a lively dance.

"What's this?" Will asked. "Fun or education?"

"Both," said the Principal. "And it's also applied ethics. Like these breathing exercises we were talking about just now—only more effective because so much more violent."

"So stamp it out," the children were chanting in unison. And they stamped their small sandaled feet with all their might. "So stamp it out!" A final furious stamp and they were off again, jigging and turning, into another movement of the dance.

"This is called the Rakshasi Hornpipe," said Mrs. Narayan.

"Rakshasi?" Will questioned. "What's that?"

"A Rakshasi is a species of demon. Very large, and exceedingly unpleasant. All the ugliest passions personified. The Rakshasi Hornpipe is a device for letting off those dangerous heads of steam raised by anger and frustration."

"So stamp it out!" The music had come round again to the choral refrain. "So stamp it out!"

"Stamp again," cried the little old lady setting a furious example. "Harder! Harder!"

"Which did more," Will speculated, "for morality and rational behavior—the Bacchic orgies or the *Republic*? the *Nichomachean Ethics* or corybantic dancing?"

"The Greeks," said Mrs. Narayan, "were much too sensible to think in terms of either-or. For them, it was always not-only-but-also. Not only Plato and Aristotle, but also the maenads. Without those tension-reducing hornpipes, the moral philosophy would have been impotent, and without the moral philosophy the hornpipers wouldn't have known where to go next. All we've done is to take a leaf out of the old Greek book."

"Very good!" said Will approvingly. Then remembering (as sooner or later, however keen his pleasure and however genuine his enthusiasm, he always did remember) that he was the man who wouldn't take yes for an answer, he suddenly broke into laughter. "Not that it makes any difference in the long run," he said. "Corybantism couldn't stop the Greeks from cutting one another's throats. And when Colonel Dipa decides to move, what will your Rakshasi Hornpipes do for you? Help you to reconcile yourselves to your fate, perhaps—that's all."

"Yes, that's all," said Mrs. Narayan. "But being reconciled to one's fate—that's already a great achievement."

"You seem to take it all very calmly."

"What would be the point of taking it hysterically? It wouldn't make our political situation any better; it would merely make our personal situation a good deal worse."

"So stamp it out," the children shouted again in unison, and the boards trembled under their pounding feet. "So stamp it out."

"Don't imagine," Mrs. Narayan resumed, "that this is the only kind of dancing we teach. Redirecting the power generated by bad feelings is important. But equally important is directing good feelings and right knowledge into expression. Expressive movements, in this case, expressive gesture. If you had come yesterday, when our visiting master was here, I could have shown you how we teach that kind of dancing. Not today unfortunately. He won't be here again before Tuesday."

"What sort of dancing does he teach?"

Mrs. Narayan tried to describe it. No leaps, or high kicks, no running. The feet always firmly on the ground. Just bending and sideways motions of the knees and hips. All expression confined to the arms, wrists and hands, to the neck and head, the face and, above all, the eyes. Movement from the shoulders upwards and outwards—movement intrinsically beautiful and at the same time charged with symbolic meaning. Thought taking shape in ritual and stylized gesture. The whole body transformed into a hieroglyph, a succession of hieroglyphs, or attitudes modulating from significance to significance like a poem or a piece of music. Movements of the muscles representing movements of Consciousness, the passage of Suchness into the many, of the many into the immanent and ever-present One.

"It's meditation in action," she concluded. "It's the metaphysics of the Mahayana expressed, not in words, but through symbolic movements and gestures."

They left the gymnasium by a different door from that through which they had entered and turned left along a short corridor.

"What's the next item?" Will asked.

"The Lower Fourth," Mrs. Narayan answered, "and they're working on Elementary Practical Psychology."

She opened a green door.

"Well, now you know," Will heard a familiar voice saying. "Nobody *has* to feel pain. You told yourselves that the pin wouldn't hurt—and it didn't hurt."

They stepped into the room and there, very tall in the midst of a score of plump or skinny little brown bodies, was Susila MacPhail. She smiled at them, pointed to a couple of chairs in a corner of the room, and turned back to the children. "Nobody *has* to feel pain," she repeated. "But never forget: pain always means that something is wrong. You've learned to shut pain off, but don't do it thoughtlessly, don't do it without asking yourselves the question: What's the reason for this pain? And if it's bad, or if there's no obvious reason for it, tell your mother about it, or your teacher, or any grown-up in your Mutual Adoption Club. *Then* shut off the pain. Shut it off knowing that, if anything needs to be done, it will be done. Do you understand? . . . And now," she went on, after all the questions had been asked and answered. "Now let's play some pretending games. Shut your eyes and pretend you're looking at that poor old mynah bird with one leg that comes to school every day to be fed. Can you see him?"

Of course they could see him. The one-legged mynah was evidently an old friend.

"See him just as clearly as you saw him today at lunchtime. And don't stare at him, don't make any effort. Just see what comes to you, and let your eyes shift—from his beak to his tail, from his bright little round eye to his one orange leg."

"I can hear him too," a little girl volunteered. "He's saying *'Karuna, Karuna!'* "

"That's not true," another child said indignantly. "He's saying 'Attention!' "

"He's saying both those things," Susila assured them. "And probably a lot of other words besides. But now we're going to do some real pretending. Pretend that there are two one-legged mynah birds. Three one-legged mynah birds. Four one-legged mynah birds. Can you see all four of them?"

They could.

"Four one-legged mynah birds at the four corners of a square, and a fifth one in the middle. And now let's make them change their color. They're white now. Five white mynah birds with yellow heads and one orange leg. And now the heads are blue. Bright blue—and the rest of the bird is pink. Five pink birds with blue heads. And they keep changing. They're purple now. Five purple birds with white heads and each of them has one pale-green leg. Goodness, what's happening! There aren't five of them; there are ten. No, twenty, fifty, a hundred. Hundreds and hundreds. Can you see them?" Some of them could—without the slightest difficulty; and for those who couldn't go the whole hog, Susila proposed more modest goals.

"Just make twelve of them," she said. "Or if twelve is too many, make ten, make eight. That's still an awful lot of mynahs. And now," she went on, when all the children had conjured up all the purple birds that each was capable of creating, "now they're gone." She clapped her hands. "Gone! Every single one of them. There's nothing there. And now you're not going to see mynahs, you're going to see *me*. One me in yellow. Two mes in green. Three mes in blue with pink spots. Four mes in the brightest red you ever saw." She clapped her hands again. "All gone. And this time it's Mrs. Narayan and that funny-looking man with a stiff leg who came in with her. Four of each of them. Standing in a big circle in the gymnasium. And now they're dancing the Rakshasi Hornpipe. 'So stamp it out, so stamp it out.' "

There was a general giggle. The dancing Wills and Principals must have looked richly comical.

Susila snapped her fingers.

"Away with them! Vanish! And now each of you sees three of your mothers and three of your fathers running round the playground. Faster, faster, faster! And suddenly they're not there any more. And then they *are* there. But next moment they aren't. They are there, they aren't. They are, they aren't . . .' "

The giggles swelled into squeals of laughter and at the height of the laughter a bell rang. The lesson in Elementary Practical Psychology was over.

"What's the point of it all?" Will asked when the children had run off to play and Mrs. Narayan had returned to her office.

"The point," Susila answered, "is to get people to understand that we're not *completely* at the mercy of our memory and our phantasies. If we're disturbed by what's going on inside our heads, we can do something about it. It's all a question of being shown what to do and then practicing, the way one learns to write or play the flute. What those children you saw here were being taught is a very simple technique—a technique that we'll develop later on into a method of liberation. Not complete liberation, of course. But half a loaf is a great deal better than no bread. This technique won't lead you to the discovery of your Buddha-Nature: but it may help you to prepare for that discovery—help you by liberating you from the hauntings of your own painful memories, your remorses, your causeless anxieties about the future."

" 'Hauntings,' " Will agreed, "is the word."

From *Education and the Significance of Life*

J. Krishnamurti

For the last fifty years, Krishnamurti has been speaking to audiences around the world, calling for a radical change in our approach to life. This Indian religious teacher has maintained a lifelong interest in the education of young people; here he presents a compelling statement of what education should be.

Only love can bring about the understanding of another. Where there is love there is instantaneous communion with the other, on the same level and at the same time. It is because we ourselves are so dry, empty and without love that we have allowed governments and systems to take over the education of our children and the direction of our lives; but governments want efficient technicians, not human beings, because human beings become dangerous to governments—and to organized religions as well. That is why governments and religious organizations seek to control education.

Life cannot be made to conform to a system, it cannot be forced into a framework, however nobly conceived; and a mind that has merely been trained in factual knowledge is incapable of meeting life with its variety,

From *Education and the Significance of Life* by J. Krishnamurti (New York: Harper & Row, 1953), pp. 23–30. Copyright 1953 by K & R Foundation. Reprinted by permission of Harper & Row, Publishers, Inc.

its subtlety, its depths and great heights. When we train our children according to a system of thought or a particular discipline, when we teach them to think within departmental divisions, we prevent them from growing into integrated men and women, and therefore they are incapable of thinking intelligently, which is to meet life as a whole.

The highest function of education is to bring about an integrated individual who is capable of dealing with life as a whole. The idealist, like the specialist, is not concerned with the whole, but only with a part. There can be no integration as long as one is pursuing an ideal pattern of action; and most teachers who are idealists have put away love, they have dry minds and hard hearts. To study a child, one has to be alert, watchful, self-aware, and this demands far greater intelligence and affection than to encourage him to follow an ideal.

Another function of education is to create new values. Merely to implant existing values in the mind of the child, to make him conform to ideals, is to condition him without awakening his intelligence. Education is intimately related to the present world crisis, and the educator who sees the causes of this universal chaos should ask himself how to awaken intelligence in the student, thus helping the coming generation not to bring about further conflict and disaster. He must give all his thought, all his care and affection to the creation of right environment and to the development of understanding, so that when the child grows into maturity he will be capable of dealing intelligently with the human problems that confront him. But in order to do this, the educator must understand himself instead of relying on ideologies, systems and beliefs.

Let us not think in terms of principles and ideals, but be concerned with things as they are; for it is the consideration of what *is* that awakens intelligence, and the intelligence of the educator is far more important than his knowledge of a new method of education. When one follows a method, even if it has been worked out by a thoughtful and intelligent person, the method becomes very important, and the children are important only as they fit into it. One measures and classifies the child, and then proceeds to educate him according to some chart. This process of education may be convenient for the teacher, but neither the practice of a system nor the tyranny of opinion and learning can bring about an integrated human being.

The right kind of education consists in understanding the child as he is without imposing upon him an ideal of what we think he should be. To enclose him in the framework of an ideal is to encourage him to conform, which breeds fear and produces in him a constant conflict between what he is and what he should be; and all inward conflicts have their outward manifestations in society. Ideals are an actual hindrance to our understanding of the child and to the child's understanding of himself.

A parent who really desires to understand his child does not look at him through the screen of an ideal. If he loves the child, he observes him, he studies his tendencies, his moods and peculiarities. It is only when one feels no love for the child that one imposes upon him an ideal, for then one's ambitions are trying to fulfill themselves in him, wanting him to become this or that. If one loves, not the ideal, but the child, then there is a possibility of helping him to understand himself as he is.

If a child tells lies, for example, of what value is it to put before him the ideal of truth? One has to find out why he is telling lies. To help the child, one has to take time to study and observe him, which demands patience, love and care; but when one has no love, no understanding, then one forces the child into a pattern of action which we call an ideal.

Ideals are a convenient escape, and the teacher who follows them is incapable of understanding his students and dealing with them intelligently; for him, the future ideal, the what should be, is far more important than the present child. The pursuit of an ideal excludes love, and without love no human problem can be solved.

If the teacher is of the right kind, he will not depend on a method, but will study each individual pupil. In our relationship with children and young people, we are not dealing with mechanical devices that can be quickly repaired, but with living beings who are impressionable, volatile, sensitive, afraid, affectionate; and to deal with them, we have to have great understanding, the strength of patience and love. When we lack these, we look to quick and easy remedies and hope for marvellous and automatic results. If we are unaware, mechanical in our attitudes and actions, we fight shy of any demand upon us that is disturbing and that cannot be met by an automatic response, and this is one of our major difficulties in education.

The child is the result of both the past and the present and is therefore already conditioned. If we transmit our background to the child, we perpetuate both his and our own conditioning. There is radical transformation only when we understand our own conditioning and are free of it. To discuss what should be the right kind of education while we ourselves are conditioned is utterly futile.

While the children are young, we must of course protect them from physical harm and prevent them from feeling physically insecure. But unfortunately we do not stop there; we want to shape their ways of thinking and feeling, we want to mould them in accordance with our own cravings and intentions. We seek to fulfill ourselves in our children, to perpetuate ourselves through them. We build walls around them, condition them by our beliefs and ideologies, fears and hopes—and then we cry and pray when they are killed or maimed in wars, or otherwise made to suffer by the experiences of life.

Such experiences do not bring about freedom; on the contrary, they strengthen the will of the self. The self is made up of a series of defensive and expansive reactions, and its fulfillment is always in its own projections and gratifying identifications. As long as we translate experience in terms of the self, the "me" and the "mine," as long as the "I," the ego, maintains itself through its reactions, experience cannot be freed from conflict, confusion and pain. Freedom comes only when one understands the ways of the self, the experiencer. It is only when the self, with its accumulated reactions, is not the experiencer, that experience takes on an entirely different significance and becomes creation.

If we would help the child to be free from the ways of the self, which cause so much suffering, then each one of us should set about altering deeply his attitude and relationship to the child. Parents and educators, by their own thought and conduct, can help the child to be free and to flower in love and goodness.

Education as it is at present in no way encourages the understanding of the inherited tendencies and environmental influences which condition the mind and heart and sustain fear, and therefore it does not help us to break through these conditionings and bring about an integrated human being. Any form of education that concerns itself with a part and not with the whole of man inevitably leads to increasing conflict and suffering.

It is only in individual freedom that love and goodness can flower; and the right kind of education alone can offer this freedom. Neither conformity to the present society nor the promise of a future Utopia can ever give to the individual that insight without which he is constantly creating problems.

The right kind of educator, seeing the inward nature of freedom, helps each individual student to observe and understand his own self-projected values and impositions; he helps him to become aware of the conditioning influences about him, and of his own desires, both of which limit his mind and breed fear; he helps him, as he grows to manhood, to observe and understand himself in relation to all things, for it is the craving for self-fulfillment that bring endless conflict and sorrow.

Surely, it is possible to help the individual to perceive the enduring values of life, without conditioning. Some may say that this full development of the individual will lead to chaos; but will it? There is already confusion in the world, and it has arisen because the individual has not been educated to understand himself. While he has been given some superficial freedom, he has also been taught to conform, to accept the existing values.

Against this regimentation, many are revolting; but unfortunately their revolt is a mere self-seeking reaction, which only further darkens our existence. The right kind of educator, aware of the mind's tendency to reaction, helps the student to alter present values, not out of reaction against them, but through understanding the total process of life. Full co-operation between man and man is not possible without the integration which right education can help to awaken in the individual.

Educators' Checklist:
Questions to Ask Ourselves about Schooling

Gay Hendricks

Sometimes the process of education seems to illustrate the classic example of not seeing the forest for the trees; we get so busy teaching the required curriculum that we forget to ask what education should really be. Here one of the editors presents a series of questions designed to stimulate a fundamental evaluation of the purpose of schooling.

1. *Am I teaching students what they most want to know?*

A survey conducted by the author asked students to rank ten subjects in order of interest. The results, ranked from most interesting (1) to least interesting (10), were as follows:

1. Sex and your sexuality
2. Getting high without drugs (meditation, body awareness, etc.)
3. Communication skills (how to talk and listen to each other)
4. Keeping yourself healthy (self-healing, physical fitness, etc.)
5. Death and dying

6. Art
7. Social studies (history, civics, political science)
8. Biology
9. Geography (natural resources, etc.)
10. Mathematics

As can be seen, the areas of greatest importance to students are rarely found in the school curriculum, while those areas in which students are relatively uninterested comprise the larger part of the curriculum. In other words, customers are being forced to go to the store to buy something they don't want. Other businesses have failed for less fundamental reasons.

Interestingly, when adults are asked to rank the same subjects, the results come out nearly identical to the students' rating. Thus, the argument that schools are teaching something that will be important later in life does not seem to be supported.

2. *Am I teaching the whole person?*

Some facets of the whole person that deserves study are:

> feelings
> fantasy
> dreams
> personal problem solving (how to dissolve arguments, etc.)
> psychic phenomena
> decision-making

There is a substantial body of knowledge available for each of the above subjects, but little use of this knowledge is being made in schools.

Poets and scientists alike have pointed out that intellect is only part of the human potential, yet the intellect continues to get the major share of attention in schools.

3. *Am I teaching processes?*

Take, for example, the memory process. Rather than having students memorize lists of things (state capitals, periodical table of elements), it might be more beneficial to teach them the process of memorization. We are always wanting to remember things like names and telephone numbers, and there are many excellent techniques available for building memory skills.

Memory is but one process; there are many others as important. In general, though, schools should be teaching *how* instead of *what*.

4. *Am I giving students information that is useful only in terms of future schooling?*

Schools teach many subjects (e.g., geometry) simply because they are prerequisites for another (e.g., trigonometry).

5. *Am I teaching students how to decondition themselves?*

Most of the things that cause people to be unhappy are due to conditioned ways of thinking, feeling, acting, and moving. Since schools, along with parents, are the major source of conditioning, some time should be spent teaching students how to get beyond their conditioning.

6. *Am I teaching students how to solve personal and interpersonal problems?*

Most problems can be solved with the following formula: feelings + wants = solution. In most problem situations an individual can ask, "How am I feeling?" (Sad? Angry? Scared?) and "What do I want to feel better?" (I want Jimmy to stop making fun of me.)

Here are a few examples:

Feeling	*Wants*
I'm angry	I want more attention from Dad.
I'm scared	I want to know that people aren't going to laugh when I read my oral report.

When one or more people have a problem, clear statements of feelings and wants can often lead to a solution.

7. *Am I teaching students how to learn?*

How do we go about finding out what we want to know? The *process* of learning can be useful to students throughout their lives.

8. *Am I teaching cultural relativity?*

Kurt Vonnegut writes, "A first-grader should understand that his or her culture isn't a rational invention; that there are thousands of other cultures and they all work pretty well; that all cultures function on faith rather than truth; that there are lots of alternatives to our own society. Cultural relativity is defensible and attractive. It's also a source of hope. It means we don't have to continue this way if we don't like it."

9. *Am I teaching students how to learn about themselves?*

How do I feel? What do I want? Who am I? How did I get the way I am?

We are the most important subject of all.

PRACTICING TRANSPERSONAL EDUCATION

Stimulated by visionaries like Krishnamurti, Aldous Huxley, and others, innovative educators began looking for ways in which transpersonal education could be implemented in the classroom. Theories are often fascinating to read, but the practicing educator needs activities that students can do today. In this section we present a wide variety of ideas and exercises which can provide the basis for a transpersonal curriculum for any classroom, K-12.

Among the areas covered in this section are dreamwork, fantasy, biofeedback, body awareness, psychic abilities, and meditation. It is our conviction that the quest for transpersonal experience must begin with a penetrating look into oneself. In the following section we present a number of tools meant to facilitate that exploration.

Dreams have poetic integrity and truth. This limbo and dust-hole of thought is presided over by a certain reason, too. Their extravagance from nature is yet within a higher nature. They seem to suggest to us an abundance and fluency of thought not familiar to waking experience.

—*Emerson*

What Would Happen to the American Psyche If, along with Homerooms, Flag Saluting and I.Q. Testing, Schools Had Daily Dream Sharing?

Patricia Pirmantgen

This article explores the fascinating world of dreams. Educators who have tried dream work in the classroom know that there is no quicker way to capture the interest of a group of students than to start them talking about their dreams. For other approaches to dreamwork, see Ann Faraday's The Dream Game, *and* The Centering Book *by Hendricks and Wills*

Patricia Pirmantgen edits a newsletter Dreams and Inner Spaces, *which offers some of the freshest ideas currently available in the field of dream work.*

We dream every night, which is analogous to having our own personal movie studio or repertory company in full-time operation. Fantastic and true, so what keeps most of us from using to advantage such fabulous facilities? Unfortunately, the snag is that we carry our culture's bias and conditioning toward the so-called irrational, so we fail to enjoy or recognize the significance of these "movies" or "dramas" that are provided, night after night, for our private viewing. Erich Fromm says it all when he calls dreams, along with myths and fairy tales, the forgotten language.[1]

While research shows that dreaming is a regular activity or state experienced by virtually all of us during sleep,[2] many people, once awake, rarely recall or work with their own dreams. When dream content does stick in the mind, the average, conditioned response is to make a vague association with Freudian psychology and/or sex; emotionally upsetting dreams (nightmares) are blamed on daytime problems or malfunction of the digestive tract.

Those dreams vivid enough to make a lasting impression still leave us at a loss for what to do with them; so dreams are shoved in the mind's unsolved mystery file, rather than being used for the direct channel they provide to one's creativity and inner space. People in our culture with some notion of how to work with their own dream content are probably met about as often as speakers of Basque or other equally exotic minorities. Even in a fairly sophisticated group, where the mention of dreams might not immediately call up that superstitious mixture of fear and fascination that things "occult" hold for Western man, a person actively involved with his own dreams would still be considered eccentric unless he could give the rationale of psychoanalysis.

Six years ago, being such a biased and conditioned American myself, I casually suggested to sixty students in creative writing that their dreams were a possible source of ideas; I mentioned dreams simply because they are vivid experiences common to everyone. That suggestion sparked an explosion of interest that led to research, experimentation and, eventually, made dream work an integral part of the teaching and curriculum writing that I do.

[1]Erich Fromm, *The Forgotten Language* (New York: Holt, Rinehart and Winston, 1951), p. 8. Fromm says, "Dreams fared even worse in the judgment of modern enlightenment. They were considered to be plain senseless, and unworthy of the attention of grown-up men, who were busy with such important matters as building machines and considered themselves 'realistic' because they saw nothing but the reality of things they could conquer and manipulate; realists who have a special word for each type of automobile, but only the one word 'love' to express the most varied kinds of affective experience."

[2]Scientists have been studying states during sleep through electrical recordings of brain and body activity. The findings show dreaming can and does happen in everyone's sleep. Even people who claim they do not dream, when awakened in the lab during REM (Rapid Eye Movement sleep) report dreams. See Related Reading for some references.

About the time my growing awareness of the significance of dreams had brought me to the point of whimsically speculating about what marvelous transformations might be made in the American psyche and culture if schools were to substitute dream sharing for I.Q. testing, I came across an article. It described a culture where dream work does play a significant and major role in the educative process and the life of a culture. The Senoi, 12,000 people living in the mountains of Malay, were visited in 1935 by a scientific expedition. The Senoi people claimed in the past two to three hundred years to have had no violent crime or intercommunal conflict. Kilton Stewart, who was in the expedition, wrote about their dream work. ". . .the absence of violent crime, armed conflict, and mental and physical diseases. . .can only be explained on the basis of. . .a high state of psychological integration and emotional maturity, along with social skills and attitudes which promote creative. . . interpersonal relations. . .Breakfast in the Senoi house is like a dream clinic, with listening to and analyzing the dreams of all the children. At the end of the family clinic the male population gathers in the council, at which the dreams. . .are reported, discussed and analyzed."[3]

Work with dreams had also led me to look again and differently at the matter of myth; here was another question to be asked, another relationship to be explored, because as two authors, Kluckhohn and Leighton, pointed out, "Folklore must be presumed to originate in the dreams and fantasies of individuals."[4] Could it be that our culture's folklore and myth are cut off from a primary source—the people's dream experiences, which express, as no think-tank or academic perspective can, what we presently term the cosmic meanings underlying human life—those same meanings that inspire art and literature? J. R. R. Tolkien once explained that he created the *Ring* series because today's English people were poor in myth. Americans suffer the same poverty; or maybe it's not that we have few myths, but that the myths we have are so bad, lacking the juices of life. Think of the myth of being male so successfully marketed by *Playboy,* or the various inane images held up as ideals in advertising or

---

[3]Stewart's article on the Senoi has been reprinted in various places; the Related Reading Section gives several sources. Stewart concludes, "In the West the thinking we do while asleep usually remains on a muddled, childish or psychotic level because we do not respond to dreams as socially important and include dreaming in the educative process."

[4]Clyde Kluckhohn and Dorothea Leighton, *The Navaho* (Cambridge: Harvard University Press, 1951), p. 136.

TV broadcasting. It seems to me we should explore whether or not our culture's exclusion of dreams from serious and creative work affects the quality of our dominant myths. It's worth pondering what kind of leaders Kennedy, Johnson and Nixon would have aspired to be if they had had the influence of different myths. We should ask whether or not there exists a relationship between dream work, our culture's dominant myths and such phenomena as drug addiction and alcoholism; conspicuous, compulsive consumption; the psychic and physical violence that is part of our culture; the rape of the ecological environment; or the prominent place we give to a kind of religion which, generally speaking, in some ways varies little from denomination to denomination and is essentially gutless, bland and devoid of qualities that uplift and inspire.

As Joseph Cambell points out, "The rise and fall of civilizations in the long, broad course of history can be seen to have been largely a function of the integrity and cogency of their supporting canons of myth; for not authority but aspiration is the motivator, builder and transformer of civilization. A mythological canon is an organization of symbols, ineffable in import, by which the energies of aspiration are evoked and gathered toward a focus."[5]

MAKING A BEGINNING

> Beginnings are not precision. Beginnings are not confusion. They are darkness drawn to a minute point of nondarkness, and silence gathered into a small sound.
> —Sheila Moon

The best place to begin is with yourself. Before trying to involve adolescents in their dreams, take time to involve yourself. For the space of two or three months, pay close attention to your own dreaming. Nightly, before going to sleep, empty your mind of the concerns of the day; clear yourself, so to speak, for dream activity. Immediately after waking, note down your dream content; if you postpone this, the dream (s) will recede from consciousness and be lost. Suggestion: record

[5]Joseph Campbell, *The Masks of God: Creative Mythology* (New York: The Viking Press, 1968), p. 5.

dreams on separate sheets, date them, keep in a file folder. Occasionally skim the collection and think about the dreams, trying to relive one or more of them. Try out some of the activities suggested later in this article for use with students. If others, teachers, friends, are interested in something of this nature, meet occasionally in a small group and share dreams.

You will notice various phenomena. For example, dreams, like movies, come in black and white or color.[6] They cover a wide range of subject matter and could be compared to the sequence of rough drafts or preliminary sketches that artists and writers go through as they clarify and refine what they are seeking to express.

At first, one's dream flow can seem without pattern, structure or coherence, but over a period of time, perhaps weeks, months or years, one finds that certain themes and motifs emerge, although from night to night they can be intermingled and mixed-up. It seems that the psyche works on several themes simultaneously, like a movie studio with many productions in process; in terms of a night's or a week's dreams, we may be seeing rushes from all the productions. Persistence in recording and working with one's dreams eventually makes it possible to tentatively group one's dreams in series on the basis of theme, setting, story or feeling values.

As a series of dreams pertaining to a theme continues, an image in it can evolve, showing itself in different ways or bringing changes in feeling in the dream self's reaction to the image. For example, a frightening dream image, such as a large, powerful dog chasing one, can go through a series of transformations from dream to dream until, while still a symbol of power, the dog image has become friendly.

It also seems that we can enter into a dream and affect its flow, so that in the case of a student who dreamed of being out in a depressing rain, not of water, but of iron balls, he could decide when next in that dream state to do something creative about the iron balls; he might catch them and build a shelter of them; he could draw a line and instruct them to fall on only one side of the line; he could call up the image of someone he trusted and ask the person for an umbrella; he could ask the sun to come out.

[6]As I've become more aware of and worked with my own dreams, the dreams themselves have become more sophisticated in their use of color. The inner dream director now uses color as a cinematographer would to create a mood, enhance a theme or convey some quality or emphasis. For visually oriented people the dream world is a rich experience.

Other phenomena you may notice: Symbols from one's religious training show up even in the dreams of those people who, consciously at least, would no longer consider themselves believers. Certain settings, people or happenings can return in dreams again and again. Extraordinarily strong feelings like terror, pain, joy and rapture can be experienced in the dream state. One's dream self may be a surprise, acting in an unexpected fashion or manifesting qualities not generally associated with oneself. Sometimes problems or matters that have consciously occupied the mind for a long time find a solution in the dream state. Much dream literature mentions the chemist Kekule, who was searching for the molecular structure of benzene; his dream of a snake with its tail in its mouth, an ancient symbol called the oroboros, was the clue leading him to the discovery that the benzene structure was a closed carbon ring.

It seems that once we show this inner dream director or filmmaker that we are serious about responding to and integrating his perspective into our conscious attitudes and judgments, a channel opens up in us. When we then refer matters like personal relationships or creative problems connected with our work to the dream director, we receive feedback that is often very much to the point, extremely helpful and sometimes something that much conscious effort and thought has not yet been able to show us.

Dreams will include what we know we know and what we know we do not know. For instance, someone who has not read ancient mythology and has no way of knowing symbols or motifs from it may find such symbols appearing in his dreams.[7] The inner dream director is also quick to incorporate recent events, experiences and discoveries into his dream continuity. Most of us, of course, are familiar with the person who is dreaming of thunder and wakes up to find a severe storm in progress.

Teachers often tell about dreams of disruptive groups, of being defied by their students. It would be interesting to write a book or article about the teaching experience which is a collection of teachers' dreams and examines them for what they imply about the contemporary educative process. In terms of helping teachers, especially in so vital an area as student-teacher relationships, dream content might be a good and basic starting point.

---

[7]Jungian psychology includes the concept of the collective unconscious, a level of the individual's psyche that does *not* derive from his personal experience but from which contents can manifest themselves.

DREAM WORK IN THE CLASSROOM
CONTEXT

> *A solution which solves a problem intellectually, moral-*
> *ly or aesthetically but not in all three modes is a false*
> *solution. The theoretical foundation for such a view is*
> *abstruse and controversial and pedagogically the task of*
> *blending in the pupil what is separated out in the culture*
> *is difficult but the need for such unification is not*
> *controversial.*
> *—Harry S. Broudy*

The process covers three areas:

1. Developing a group's awareness, recognition and memory of dream states and content.
2. Creative work with their own dream material.
3. Drawing parallels between dream content and the English curriculum.

Work on dreams usually has to be a peripheral part of a curriculum, but it's not hard, I find, even with limited time to build a group's involvement. People generally are fascinated by anything pertaining to themselves and the occasional sharing of dreams and some creative work with them has been sufficient to hold interest and provide momentum for a group process to evolve.

Developing Awareness[8]

Begin by sharing an interesting dream of your own; make its images come alive as you retell it and try to communicate something of the emotional impact that it had on you. This will usually be enough to remind the group of dreams of their own that they want to talk about. Even those who retain little or no memory of dream activity at night will have had at least one dream make a lasting impression. The dream sharing stimulates memories and the session isn't long enough to include everything students are reminded of, so they leave, reluctantly, still talking.

[8]In my experience today's students are intensely interested in whatever pertains to their inner space. *"Star Trek"* re-runs, science fiction, the drug culture, meditation techniques like TM, etc., have made them curious about altered states of consciousness; they are genuinely interested in working with their dreams.

This first mention of dreams usually calls up two sets of reactions: [some students] are immediately interested or at least curious and [some students] say they do not dream. The following steps help people with either reaction grow more aware of their own dream activity, especially carrying some memory of it over into waking consciousness.

A.   Before going to sleep, think of the mind as a chalkboard. Wipe it clear of daytime stuff; let sleep come. Or think of the mind as a TV or movie screen where nothing is now being projected; the screen is empty, waiting for the dream images to be projected on it.

B.   In the morning, immediately after waking up, take five minutes to write or tape whatever details of dreams are still on the screen, i.e., remembered. Don't give up because there is nothing there the first few mornings. Persistence, eventually, will bring results.

Once a week or every other week set aside a regular time to share something from recent dreams. Tell one or more of your own that are appropriate; someone who has had a frightening dream may be relieved . . . if he sees that others also have them. At first, some will be shy, but if there is an accepting/enjoying tone to the sessions, reticences gradually dissolve and in time everyone is vying for a turn. Within weeks (three to seven in my experience), the "non-dreamers" discover themselves dreaming. Several side effects of the process eventually become noticeable: those who thought themselves uncreative and lacking in imagination begin to feel they do have creative talents. The group process and exchange grow closer to true democracy with differences such as race, social class and verbal ability no longer such barriers or the sole basis of their response to each other. They also begin to find more meaning in the traditional content of English and composition work.

After the process is on-going and there is real interest in dreams, I mingle the dream-sharing with simple activities like the following:

The group goes through the letters of the alphabet giving words that begin with each letter (abacus, butter, calluses, etc.). Then each one, using this word list, makes up a story; everyone reads his or her stories aloud. Or we take a group of typical images that come in dreams (flower, mountain, house, mysterious stranger, road) and with them create a story or an outline for a film.[9]

The point of these activities is to give the group experience in creating where the conscious, planning part of themselves works along with the

---

[9]These stories can sometimes be surprisingly coherent and interesting; for the student who thinks writing impossible they can be a breakthrough.

unknown part of themselves, that mysterious aspect of the self from which dreams may also flow. As we discuss the stories and the method by which they were created, several questions are explored:

* Did I know this story was in me before I wrote it?
* Where did it come from?
* Could I have written it without the list of words?
* Could we speculate that something akin to this happens in dreaming—a presently unknown source or power within ourselves creates "movies" that consciously we don't know are in us?
* Is the key to creative writing in a combination of conscious work, materials and finding a way to open the flow from that unknown source or power in oneself?

At this point in the process, I might plan a creative writing project which will draw on their own dreams for content. I am careful, however, not to give creative work related to dreams until I see that they are really interested and involved.

The first time doing dream work with a group, it's well to limit the activity to the simple and regular sharing of dreams. If teachers go slowly, gradually coming to an intuitive grasp of the process rather than trying too much too soon, they will be able to nuture the process and bring it to a fruit-bearing stage. But if we get all excited and involved ourselves with dreams, it's tempting to flood students with our newly acquired information and enthusiasm. That can be harmful because it may block the way to the students' own discovery of meaning in dream work; it's best not to share a lot, initially, of what we know about dreams, but to wait until questions come that show a readiness, a context for taking in what we have to give.

One more caution: In group work of this sort the content is being generated by teacher and students, which implies the need for a healthy group dynamic, a real relationship between the teacher and the group. For the kind of sharing that's involved here, people have to be to a degree open, trusting, enjoying and accepting of themselves and others. However, it should be noted that the very process of dream sharing seems to help create the kind of atmosphere that is needed.

Creative Work

There are many ways of proceeding here. Create your own or select from the following on the basis of inclination, group interest, need.

ACTIVITIES:

   A.   Keep a dream diary or journal. Record dreams in it, dating them, putting down the details that are remembered or the feelings they held. Occasionally, review the dream diary; look for images or themes that repeat themselves, that are evolving and changing. Work with and amplify such images; see H. for the process.

   B.   Dreams can be re-created as short stories, as films or filmstrips or as continuity for short, experimental dramas. A group might select from their dreams several to weave together in dramatic form. Groups could present their plays to each other.

   C.   Some dream images make striking posters. Combine efforts with the art and/or photography departments.

   D.   Role-play, using the dream material as a starting point for a character or a situation. Ask the student whose dream it is to select group members to act it out with him. This is a beginning way of probing dream content for meaning, of interpreting the dream.

   E.   Create a dialogue between one's waking self and one of the dream characters.

   F.   In writing or in cartooned sequences continue the dream from its last remembered scene. Or create variations of it.

   G.   Write descriptions of unusual dream characters or dream settings.

   H.   Work with some of the dream images, amplifying their meaning by building up a web of related associations. For example, in one group after several students had had houses in their dreams, we took down everything we could think of concerning houses—openings such as doors and windows; many rooms with different purposes such as a kitchen where things were cooked, closets with things hidden in them, the bathroom, halls linking rooms to each other. We noted that houses could have levels from underground basements to dusty, seldom entered attics. There were places in houses that were little used; there were rooms or furnishings that received much use. A house itself was a container in which more than one life process was happening—birth, growth, conflict, love. A child living in a house would not know everything that went on within its walls. A grown-up might have forgotten much that had gone on within it; he might be ignorant of its past, unable to predict its future. We recalled literary associations such as the house of Usher. We remembered different houses from our dreams and experiences that we had had with houses. Then we made the transition from a house as a house to a house as a symbol of image for one's own self or being, paralleling all the items we had noted for houses with possible equivalents in the human life or psyche.

   Such brainstorming sessions in which everyone shares associations with a symbol or image are helpful in several ways. They show how to begin to extract meaning from a dream and they develop the students' intellectual and emotional comprehension of images and symbols, no matter what the context-film, poetry, novels or dreams.

After the group just mentioned had worked with the images of house, dog, cat and tree, a girl came one day, excited and curious about a dream of washing machines. The group went to work on the image and in five minutes the chalkboard was filled with associations related to washing machines.

While a dictionary of symbols is helpful for the teacher, it is best not to bring it into the classroom for several reasons. Although there is a universal meaning that attaches to or is communicated by symbols, the person who has had a dream is the one best suited to know what its images mean for him. But for students and for most of us, so far as meaning goes, our dreams are puzzles, seemingly beyond figuring out. Carl Jung says a dream is a hint and to unlock its meaning we have to fill out the implications of the hint. The work the group did with the images of the house and the washing machines was that kind of filling out. When a group amplifies enough dream images together, they learn how to exercise the skill for themselves; if they look up symbols in a dictionary, they will miss out on valuable practice and experience. Also, when they work with a dream image, they are grappling with the dream content; if they go to a dictionary, they may come away with information but they will not necessarily have acquired a personal understanding of their own dream content.

Drawing Parallels Between Dream Content and the English Curriculum

It should not be necessary to modify much whatever is one's present curriculum; there is such a wealth of possibilities in the area of English and the humanities. Much poetry; a novel like *Moby Dick,* the work of Shakespeare; themes such as hero, conflict, courage; authors like Faulkner, Conrad, Frost, Blake; the world of myth; many contemporary films—all begin to take on new significance for a group when dream work is integrated with their reading, writing and discussion. The students see themselves in dreams experiencing the same mythic, weird, mysterious, emotionally charged worlds and situations that are the stuff of fiction and poetry. In becoming more conscious of their own dreams, they have found a reason to identify. They have also discovered how difficult it is to communicate these complex states and experiences. Since social recognition is more or less denied inner states, we presently lack a commonly accepted nomenclature or working concepts to readily make our dream states intelligible to each other. But often in lyric poetry, in some section of a novel or play, or in a scene from a film, we can catch a glimpse of something that reminds us of a dream experience.

I would also speculate that the level of the psyche where dreams originate is akin to the level of stratum of the psyche where creative works are initiated.[10] The students, in making conscious contact with that level in themselves, are sensitized, are put in touch through empathy with the creative experience and emotional states expressed in literature and film. An awareness of this adds to the intellectual study of literature a feeling dimension that helps students grasp the texture or flavor of a particular piece. Students begin to catch the shimmer of significant meaning in literature; they learn to feel respect and appreciation for a literary heritage that previously may have seemed to them little more than irrelevant deadwood.

It seems to me that, properly handled, dream work in the context of the English class is an area, a place, a way to achieve a real integration of the affective and the cognitive domains in the educative process.

CLOSING THOUGHTS

No one should make the mistake of assuming this article covers the full range of potential and possibility that is implied by dream states and their content. There are many aspects of the dream experience and questions concerning what really does happen in the state of dreaming that are not touched upon here.

It should be mentioned that much of today's literature on dreams comes, of course, from various schools of psychiatric thought; while the English teacher will have to rely on this for help, it is necessary to keep in mind that dreaming is an activity of the healthy psyche as well as the disturbed psyche; the psychoanalytic perspective suffers inevitable distortion because it is one that thinks primarily in terms of disturbance, unhealth and disease; it is wise, therefore, not to make blanket applications of psychoanalytic insights or to take them for infallible and universal truths. The various schools of thought do not yet themselves agree upon such basics as the origin of dream activity and the interpretation of dream content.

---

[10] R.L. Stevenson, Blake, Poe, Coleridge, Mozart and Saint-Saens are a few to consciously draw on dream activity for creative work.

We are just at the start of systematic study of the various aspects of dream activity, but some interesting and provocative physiological data has already emerged. For example, in his book, *Dreams and the Growth of Personality,* growth therapist Ernest Rossi summarizes data that give support to the view, he says, that new protein structures are actually being synthesized in the brain during the dream state. Dr. Rossi says, "These new organic structures are the forerunners of creative change in our view of ourselves and the world. They are the biological foundation of a naturally occurring process of constructive change in our personalities and behavior."[11]

Dr. Rossi, like many others writing on dreams, has had training in the Jungian perspective on the human psyche. It is my experience that an English, humanities or media teacher beginning dream work will find more help in the writings of people trained in the Jungian school than in the works of people from the Freudian school.[12]

Dream work in the classroom does not call for elaborate materials or textbooks; it's little more than the age-old teaching process of the log with the master at one end and the student at the other. Dream work can be easily and creatively integrated into most English or humanities curriculum. It ties in particularly well, of course, with film; so well that I sometimes ask myself whether or not the development of film is an outward projection of certain inner psychic processes and space/time relationships that operate at some level within us but that we are presently not cognizant of.

The goal in the classroom is to build a conscious, responsible and accepting attitude toward one's dreams and to try to use them as a channel to one's creativity. The work with dreams in the classroom context will not be able to reduce the dream experience to a verbalized kernel that makes a definitive statement about the meaning or message of a dream; nevertheless, some feeling and intuitive understanding of dream content will develop as students work with and re-create their own dreams. The students also find in the experience a valuable freedom to

[11]Ernest Rossi, *Dreams and the Growth of Personality* (New York: Pergamon Press, Inc., 1972).

[12]George Steiner said, in an interview printed in *Psychology Today* (February, 1975), about Jung: "The more I try to structure a model for translation for the way we move from language to language via images and symbols, the more I find in Jung suggestions of extraordinary interest. It looks as if Jung, more deeply than Freud, understood the whole problem of the nature of universality—not in the Chomskian sense, but in the way that language creates fictions, creates life lies, creates complex symbols. . . . I believe that Jung is going to loom larger and larger in the tradition."

take seriously this aspect of themselves. It could even be that such explorations of their own inner space as take place when working with dreams may be a factor to help students decide against trying to alter consciousness through the use of drugs. Dream states themselves can be so rich and varied that a student might say of drugs, "Who needs them?"

There are depths hinted at and mysteries about the nature of space, time and being in dreams which centuries of thought and effort have still not answered, or perhaps the answers were once known and later lost. Apparently, judging from Biblical passages and other ancient literature such as the Greek myths and healing rites connected to the god Asklepius, dreams were considered significant by more than one society and used in healing, in religious rites and in decision-making. Remember the Pharaoh who stored grain against a famine predicted in a dream. It may well be that in taking an interest in dreams, as groups and individuals are, today, we are working our way back to a lost wisdom or art.[13]

No occasional and peripheral work such as that suggested in this article is going to completely unravel the meanings, both individual and collective, that dreams hint at, but work such as this is of much importance because it helps people open themselves to an area of their own being which is rich in meaning and probably closely allied to one's creative talents. The work gives respect to rather than ignoring a vital area of activity, for almost one-third of man's life is spent in sleep. To re-apply Shakespeare, ". . . who knows what dreams may come?" Could the American psyche be transformed if, along with homerooms and I.Q. tests, American schools were to have daily dream work?

RELATED READING

CIRLOT, J.E., *A Dictionary of Symbols*. New York: Philosophical Library, 1962. (Also available in paperback. Thus far the only symbol dictionary in one volume that I have found to be worth having.)

FARADAY, DR. ANN, *Dream Power*. New York: Berkley Medallion, 1972. (Paperback. The author's personal experience with various schools of dream analysis; the eclectic approach she worked out for herself.)

FROMM, ERICH, *The Forgotten Language*. New York: Holt, Rinehart and Winston, 1951. (On myth, dreams and fairy tales.)

---

[13]Stanley Krippner, head of the Maimonides Dream Laboratory in New York, was reported to be on the West Coast in 1973 to help set up a dream curriculum for the college level.

HALL, CALVIN S. and NORDBY, VERNON J., *The Individual and His Dreams.* New York: Signet, 1972. (Paperback. A how-to-analyze-your-own-dreams book. Hall and Nordby have studied more than 50,000 dreams and move beyond the approach of traditional psychoanalysis in their treatment of dream content, but they occasionally betray the usual biases of the American scientist.)

JUNG, CARL G., ed., *Man and His Symbols.* New York: Dell Publishing Co., Inc. 1964. (Paperback; also available in hard cover but it's considerably more expensive. Jung's works are generally not easy to read but this one has been designed for the general public. Jung's dream insights are especially helpful for anyone beginning to take the dream world seriously.)

KRIPPNER, STANLEY and HUGHES, WILLIAM, "Genius at Work," in *Psychology Today* (June 1970), pp. 40-43. (A brief article on the relationship between dreams and creativity. Also other articles on dreaming in this issue of PT.)

MAHONEY, MARIA F., *The Meaning in Dreams and Dreaming.* New York, Citadel Press, 1966. (Paperback. A Jungian approach to dreams for use by an individual working on his own; a helpful book with which to make a beginning.)

PIRMANTGEN, PATRICIA, *Dreams and Inner Spaces,* Edendale P.O., Box 26556, Los Angeles, Calif. 90026. (A recently formed non-commercial publishing company which is developing inexpensive materials related to: dreams, altered states of consciousness, mystical states, creativity, intuitive modes. Sample copy of the *Dreams and Inner Spaces* newsletter available at no charge; please send SASE, #10 size.)

ROBERTS, JANE, *The Education of Oversoul Seven.* Englewood Cliffs, N.J.: Prentice-Hall, 1972. (A science-fiction novel which revolves around manifestations in the dream world and the concept of simultaneous reincarnation. The insights regarding dreams in this book go much further than Jung, Hall, Faraday, Fromm, etc.)

ROSSI, ERNEST LAWRENCE, *Dreams and the Growth of Personality.* New York: Pergamon Press, Inc., 1972. (A fascinating book to read in that it contains the odyssey, largely expressed in dreams and visions, of a young woman in analysis with Dr. Rossi.)

TART, CHARLES T., ed. *Altered States of Consciousness.* Garden City, New York: Doubleday Anchor, 1969. (Paperback. The section on dream consciousness contains five articles. Tart's introduction to the section briefly surveys the published literature on studies and experiments related to dream states.)

WALCOTT, WILLIAM, ed., *Psychological Perspectives,* Volume 3, Number 2 (Fall 1972). (A periodical publication of the C. G. Jung Institute of Los Angeles. This issue contains a special section of four articles on dreams and dreaming. One of the four is an article on the Senoi Tribe and their use of dreams, by Kilton Stewart. The same article also appears in Tart's book. Single issues available for $2.75. Address: 595 E. Colorado Blvd., Pasadena, Calif. 91101).

Ways of Teaching

John Blofeld

John Blofeld traveled in the interior of China in the decades before the 1949 Communist revolution. These remarks were made to him by a Taoist monk who had been a prominent banker before retiring to a small, quite obscure monastery in the country.

The younger recluses here and the three young boys receive teaching from us elders. Good, but we do not set about it by laying down what they, as Taoists, must study. Instead, we start by observing our pupils, leading them on to reveal what is in their minds and to display what talents and bents belong to them naturally. Then, by whatever means come to hand, we guide each along the lines he is best fitted to follow, often learning more than we impart. What wonders would be wrought and what tragic failures avoided if schoolmasters did the same! Sooner or later, our pupils come to study the works of such sages as Laotzu, Chuangtzu and Lichtzu—not because they must, but because they grow

"Ways of Teaching." From John Blofeld, *Beyond the Gods: Buddhist and Taoist Mysticism* (New York: E. P. Dutton & Co., Inc., 1974), p. 58.

curious about the sources of our ideas. If they had no tendency that way, the young recluses would not have come here in the first place. Even so, just *how* we teach them depends not on our own preferences but on the pupils' natural aptitudes and inclinations.

It's just the way I'd always imagined it would be.

Learning through Fantasy

Frances Vaughan Clark

Guided fantasy is a useful learning tool and it has another appeal: it's fun. With a combination like that, it is amazing that educators have only recently discovered the use of fantasy techniques. Frances Vaughan Clark, a pioneer in the use of fantasy in the classroom, provides a helpful introduction to this area of transpersonal education.

Fantasy is the use of imagination in the creation of mental images. Fantasy may be either voluntary or involuntary. It can be used as a tool for creativity, for piecing together unrelated facts, for overcoming obstacles, and for experimenting with new ways of being in the world. The young child needs no instruction in the uses of fantasy. It arises spontaneously as a means of integrating the vast amount of learning which takes place during the early years. The importance of fantasy in the development of the human mind and spirit is readily accepted by artists, writers, and others who contribute to the make-believe world of childhood. When a child goes to school, however, he is expected to begin to learn about the real world, and put away the rich imaginings of his early years. Nevertheless, fantasy remains an important part of play and creativity at every age. When we reminisce, daydream, or imagine anything real or unreal, we are using fantasy. We experience fantasy journeys spontaneously every day whenever we speculate about "What if . . ." The fantasy journeys we will be discussing are not so spontaneous. They are planned, triggered by a stimulus for a particular purpose, and provide for the integration of the experience into everyday life. The ability to use fantasy and imagination is an essential part of any creative endeavor, whether it be in artistic expression or scientific discovery. Everyone is called on to solve problems in life, and no matter what the person's vocation, the ability to find imaginative alternatives and creative solutions is an asset. A student who has experienced his own creative ability will have an asset that he can call upon in any future endeavor.

Teachers, parents, or counselors who are interested in opening up the world of fantasy for exploration by children should not overlook the fact that they too may benefit personally from the experience. Adults need not remain detached observers. On the contrary, they can be better guides if they themselves have experienced the power and excitement of participating fully in a fantasy journey. Fantasy is a tool for human growth and development which is effective and rewarding at any age. Its value has long been recognized in psychotherapy, but more recently techniques derived from Jung's active imagination, DeSoilles' guided daydream, and Assagioli's psychosynthesis have been introduced into education with very positive results. Here we are not concerned with therapy, but with the development and growth of the healthy personality. Many adults need psychotherapy because their education failed to give them a sense of self-worth and the ability to take responsibility for their lives. Education which does not teach students how to use their inner resources is incomplete. Education of the whole person needs to recognize the importance of subjective as well as objective learning and to integrate inner experience with the outer reality of the environment. Learning through fantasy is one way in which this integration can take place.

Recent physiological findings indicate that our brains function in two ways. The function of the left hemisphere of the brain is predominantly linear, rational, and verbal. The function of the right hemisphere is predominantly holistic, intuitive, and metaphoric. Most of our educational process is geared to the development of left-hemisphere functions, even though we know that the greatest achievements of the human mind require the integrated functioning of both hemispheres. The ability of the right cerebral hemisphere to perceive patterns and possibilities, meaning and relationship, and to create symbolic images is essential both to the creative process and the development of the healthy personality. Yet we are only beginning to recognize the importance of validating these functions within our educational system.

What Jerome Bruner called left-handed knowing in 1962 (Bruner, J., *On Knowing: Essays For the Left Hand.* New York: Atheneum, 1962) is what we now refer to as right-hemisphere knowing, since the right hemisphere of the brain controls the left side of the body, while the left hemisphere of the brain controls the right side of the body. Although the importance of both modes of knowing has been affirmed in learning theory, the primary focus of learning theorists such as Piaget and Bruner has been on the cognitive functions of the left cerebral hemisphere.

One way of including the development of right-hemisphere functions in the educational process is through the introduction of fantasy as a valid and exciting way of learning. Recent evidence indicates that children who do not daydream are more likely to become emotionally disturbed than children who do daydream. Night dreams are also important for the maintenance of mental health, and often serve as a source of creative inspiration. By encouraging the development of fantasy thinking we can help students learn to value those subjective, visual, and artistic processes which are so important in the development of full human potential.

The kind of learning provided by altered states of consciousness such as dreams, meditation, and guided fantasy is an essential part of education for the whole person. Moreover, this type of experimental learning gives us direct access to right-cerebral functioning. By giving students the opportunity to explore their inner resources of inventiveness and creativity, affirming the importance of divergent as well as convergent thinking, we are also encouraging initiative and self-reliance. In *The Crack in the Cosmic Egg,* Joseph Pierce points out how we create our reality by the way we structure our perceptions of the world. We are now beginning to understand how a limited imagination structures reality in such a way as to prevent discovery of personal power and the assumption of responsibility for change and growth in one's own life. Learning to create a subjective reality in fantasy can also lead to a new appreciation of our capacity to change and restructure our perceptions of reality in order to allow a broader perspective on human experience and human potentials.

The use of fantasy also allows students to learn by using a variety of modalities in addition to the rational, verbal, literary approach to learning. Some students learn more quickly when visual images are evoked. Others respond more readily to such modalities as touch, texture, or kinesthetic imagery. In fantasy all the sensory modalities may be brought to bear on the experience. Sights, sounds, sensations, emotions, and thought processes are all called into play as an integral part of the process. Sometimes a teacher or guide may wish to introduce movement into the fantasy by, for instance, asking children to curl up small while imagining that they are a seed, and to stretch up as they begin to imagine themselves as a growing plant.

The importance of training the imagination as a specific psychological function has been discussed by Roberto Assagioli in *Psychosynthesis*. It is easy to see that as a person learns to take responsibility for overcoming obstacles in fantasy, where anything is possible, he is actually learning about his capacity for solving problems, overcoming obstacles, and making decisions in his life. He is also learning that he can voluntarily choose to control his own thoughts, or to relinquish control and allow spontaneous imagery to emerge. Improved self-image, increased sense of responsibility for oneself, improved ability to concentrate, and a greater appreciation and acceptance of individual differences are some of the changes which tend to be associated with learning through fantasy.

In order to create optimum conditions for increasing self-reliance and self-esteem through the experiential appreciation of inner resources, it is necessary to establish an environment of trust. Fantasies should therefore not be evaluated, interpreted, or rewarded in any way. In fantasy each individual is expanding the frontiers of his awareness and exploring the unknown by creating and combining objects, situations, and occurrences which have never existed before. Such exploration is intrinsically satisfying, and needs no secondary reinforcement. In fact, secondary reinforcement only tends to diminish interest and genuine spontaneity.

In the world of fantasy we are truly limited only by a lack of imagination. Unfortunately, the development of imagination is frequently stunted early in life when it is referred to derogatorily as "only imagination." Sometimes a good deal of practice and encouragement is needed, particularly with adults and older children, before self-imposed limitations can be discarded and the inner wellsprings of creativity can be unblocked. As a person learns to transcend the boundaries of a limited imagination the process becomes more and more enjoyable and rewarding. With increased practice, the participant may be willing to risk more in his fantasies and begin to experiment with changing self-image. For example, if he always sees himself as a heroic figure in his fantasies, and this stance is neither praised nor criticized, he may also be able to explore in fantasy his feelings of being timid or scared. Exploring alternate roles and ways of being in the world through fantasy is another aspect of learning which can have lasting effects on the individual by making him more aware of alternatives and his capacity for making choices.

By allowing participants to respond in any way they want, and make their own observations about the process, the teacher can create an atmosphere of trust and acceptance which is essential for this type of learning experience. By maintaining a non-judgmental attitude the teacher is also modeling behavior for other students who may not, at first, know how to respond. In sharing a fantasy a person always reveals something about how he feels about himself and his creations. If he becomes deeply involved, he may experience the fantasy as something which shapes itself of its own accord. The process of allowing imagery to unfold involves what we call passive volition. By this we mean simply maintaining an attitude of willing receptivity to the fantasy experience. Excessive attempts at control and conscious formulation frequently interfere with the emergence of imagery, and it is therefore recommended that fantasy journeys be preceded by a period of physical and mental relaxation. Each and every participant gets to be the director, producer, star, and audience at every show, and there is always something new to be discovered. Right now, use your fantasy: imagine how you want to guide your first fantasy journey.

How Three Teachers Use Fantasy Journeys

Richard Meznarich,
Robert Habes,
Claudia Binter

Readers who want to explore the use of fantasy for fun and personal growth are encouraged to turn to DeMille's delightful Put Your Mother on the Ceiling *and to* The Centering Book *by Hendricks and Wills.*

Here, however, three creative teachers show how fantasy can be used in several different areas of the traditional academic curriculum.

RICHARD MEZNARICH:
TEACHING ELECTRONICS
THEORY THROUGH FANTASY

I took my beginning electronics class on a [fantasy] trip into that mysterious land of invisible magnetic and electric fields surrounding the windings and core of a transformer. The procedure was as follows.

The room was darkened and the students put their heads down on the desks and were told to relax and empty their minds. They were told they were going on a trip into an electromagnetic field. Prior to beginning the journey a relaxation exercise was performed to get everyone into a totally relaxed state. Unfortunately, with dirty tile floors we could not lie down so we had to settle for sitting at the desks. Everyone was told to imagine himself or herself as an electron and to concentrate on what it might feel like to be such an incredibly small piece of negative matter. They were told to consider the world around them and to imagine what it looked like. Most of the students said they felt like planet earth compared to the universe in size relationships and they visualized everything in very rapid motion. Huge swirls of gas were constantly battering them from side to side as they traveled throughout the universe.

The students were then told they were to encounter two very large coils of wire and around the wire there was a huge and rapidly changing force field. They were to enter the force field and feel the effects of it. They were then the electrons within the coil of wire as they were affected by the rapidly changing force field which is the electromagnetic field. After allowing them to spend time adrift within the field, I told the students that another coil of equal size and strength was coming toward them, that the two fields were interacting, and that the interaction would become very violent the closer the coils came to each other. The students were told that the increase in strength of one coil caused an increase in the strength of the other coil. This produced a super-strong force which moved the electrons (the students) very fast until the electromagnetic interacting forces ceased to interact.

When the fields no longer were in existence the students felt calm and then we went into a waking period. At the end of the waking period a small light was turned on and the experience was discussed. Surprisingly, most students agreed upon what they had felt. For example, when they were told to enter the coil, they all said they felt confined despite their size. When the second coil came to interact with the first coil, most of the students felt as if a tropical storm was occurring, except that it didn't rain. They said it was more like a huge violent multicolored stream of gas clouds swirling around them, something like being on a strange planet. Only one student did not want to enter the force field and he said he just stayed in space where it was calm. One other student fell asleep and we had to awaken him.

The time for the entire trip was thirty minutes. Most students did not feel that it was that short. They felt the trip had been at least an hour long.

Since the purpose of the trip was to gain understanding of an electromagnetic field and interaction of two fields, it remained to see how well we had done. The next day the students read the chapter in the book dealing with the inductive coils. The students said they had no trouble visualizing the forces described in the book and their qualitative work in the lab seemed to bear this out. It is quite evident to me that the trip was worth taking since I have taught this subject matter before but not with this much success. What remains to be done now, of course, is to teach the material again to two different sections of the class, using both methods, and then compare the results. At any rate, it was and is interesting, for there must be a better way to teach than the centuries-old lecture method.

ROBERT HABES:
USING FANTASY IN THE
ELEMENTARY CLASSROOM

Because of the supply of methods presented in transpersonal psychology, I was able to assemble a little unit in the area. I was able to teach subject areas also. The following is an outline of each method along with some evaluations or conclusions. With few exceptions all projects were done in my sixth-grade class.

The first idea I tried was using a candle for meditation. We were challenged to create images or let the mind roam as we concentrated upon the flame of a candle. From this point we quickly jotted down what we came up with. Then the most "powerful" phrases were circled, edited, and written in poetic form; this idea was adapted from "Do You Have a Dream for English?" Although I was skeptical about such a large class trying this, I had few problems, and enthusiasm for other projects was generated. Two important points were worth observing. First, the creative images which were produced surprised even the students in retrospect. No individual had an "intellectual" advantage. Second, it may be that there is great creative capacity within all of us; only the ability to fetch it up and give it meaning differs from individual to individual. The ability to give meaning to creativity may be easier to learn than we might imagine.

The students were dramatically proud of their efforts, and we concluded with a display of their work. A reinforcement for poetry may finally be at hand.

My next endeavor was that of a fantasy journey. I made a relaxation tape recording, then taped a journey similar to the "mountain" journey.* As I made the tape I tried to include as many non-specifics as possible. Examples include: "See what you can see . . . something glowing . . . get rid of it [I didn't say how]. . .enter the opening [some did not see caves]. . .figure of *someone* [a large variety of answers]. . .how do you feel?" The class was excited at the differences in experiences, and many were quite proud of the uniqueness of a particular image. The results of such an experience are intangible and difficult to measure. One can only observe and draw conclusions, hoping to be as objective as possible. It seemed almost immediately that the class was better able to get themselves into a frame of mind suitable for thought or work. There is one reality which I cannot deny, however. Any teacher will attest to the rigors of Fridays. Following the first Thursday fantasy we had the best Friday I have ever experienced.

During the next fantasy journey I discovered that unspecific sounds create wonderful images. An airplane passed overhead while I was tape recording the journey in preparation for class. Since it seemed to fit the dialog, I increased the volume to pick it up. When the students listened to the tape in class, they saw waves, trains, planes, and planets. During this second fantasy my goal was to evoke physical and emotional feelings. Those included: "You are disappearing . . . only a thought remains . . . drift around . . . feel better than you ever felt before in your life . . . running faster . . . leaving the ground . . . flying over treetops . . . faster . . . earth disappears . . . you are becoming light itself . . . filling up your body. . .full circle. . .coming back."

I have been overwhelmed by the willingness and ability of the children to remain completely still, without a motion, for thirty minutes. Six months ago I would have laughed at the idea. Peter S———, an extremely active child, seems calmed down considerably. He also gets down to work much more quickly.

---

*A fantasy journey in which the students are led (imaginatively) up a mountain to a cave, then instructed to go inside for an adventure.

We had a discussion about dreams and what possible bearing they have on our lives. We talked about the directed dreams of Malayan children and the different ways in which dreams could be better remembered or evoked.* During all of our talks the class was in a state which only elementary teachers really understand: all eyes on whomever the speaker was, no outside interruptions, mouths open. Once started, it is amazing how eagerly children want to look inward and learn about themselves.

In an effort to make these efforts coincide with our district curriculum, I grasped at ways to include certain subject matter in the fantasy journey. Finally I hit upon taking a fantasy journey over the geographic regions of the Soviet Union. Actually, this journey lends itself to some really fascinating imagery including: "Feel the cold of the earth . . . frozen just below the surface of the earth (tundra) . . . soaring over the forests from coast to coast . . . a green wave . . . feel dry warmth of the desert . . . sand between your feet . . . soar above the snow-capped mountains." Four days after this journey I put four objective questions about the regions on a quiz. Nearly all students got these questions right even though I had not reinforced this trip or any of the concepts. Obviously, the students had a visual picture.

CLAUDIA BINTER:
FANTASY IN THE FIRST GRADE

Whenever I ask the children to write a story, I always hear "I don't know what to write." I feel that all of us are creative, but it is a matter of knowing how to get at our creativity and use it. Fantasy trips are an experience which teachers can use to help solve this problem. I asked the children to find a space on the floor, lie down, and we went through a relaxation period of about seven minutes. Their reaction to this was one of giggling. Only about four of the children were seriously taking part. I guided them along a beach, walking along, feeling the water and sand. They then found an object on the beach, picked it up, looked at it and felt it. Afterwards we discussed their experiences. What they did, how the sand and water felt, what they found in the sand, and what they did with their object were all questions I asked.

*See the section on Senoi dream work in *The Centering Book*.

The second time I tried a fantasy trip with the class, the children were much more responsive. There was not the silliness during the relaxation period that I had observed previously. I asked them to stand at the bottom of a mountain looking up. They were to climb the path which led up the mountain. I asked them to stop suddenly before a cave and then go in. They were to see something in the cave, then climb back down the mountain. This time I asked them to write about their experience. One child exclaimed, "I'm going to need about three pages to tell everything I did!" This type of preparation before a creative writing session is very beneficial. Their story is something they have just experienced, and the image is fresh in their minds. Through the use of visual imagery, creative writing is much more successful, and it also avoids the frustration of not knowing what to say.

To try a slightly different approach to the fantasy trip, I asked the children to find a space on the floor and proceeded with a short relaxation period. After the session they were asked to remain in the same position while listening to the record *Peter and the Wolf*. The record tells the story but leaves time for the children to use their imaginations and visualize the scenes during the interval of music. The children were relaxed and quietly listened to the music and story. Afterwards, I asked them to show me what they had seen and felt during the record through the medium of fingerpaints. I told them that if they had been thinking about something other than the story, to show that. I also played the record over again while they were fingerpainting. Most of the children worked quietly: if they spoke, it was in a whisper. The children are always in a rush when doing any art project, but they were much more relaxed during this project and took their time. They seemed to enjoy it more. Afterwards I discussed the picture with the individual child. Most of them drew pictures which were related to the story. However, one child pictured the duck eating the wolf instead of the wolf eating the duck. There were a few children who painted pictures that were not related to the story.

Many of the ways in which transpersonal psychology can be used are not applicable to a first-grade classroom. However, there are transpersonal experiences which would be very profitable for the young, such as dreams and the use of fantasy trips. If personal awareness is to be fully achieved by an individual, it should begin at an early age in order that the individual may function at a higher level by the time he reaches adulthood.

From *Psychic Development*

Jean Porter

The area of psychic phenomena seems to be universally interesting. In this article, Jean Porter dispels the notion that this is a mysterious faculty possessed by only a few, arguing, instead, that all of us possess untapped potential for what she calls NSP—normal sense perception. Jean, who had her psychic abilities awakened through techniques like those in this article, now teaches classes on psychic development in Berkeley.

There are several reasons why I have written this as well as why I teach classes in psychic development. One is to dispel the mystique of the psychic and remove superstitious and spooky interpretations of its function in our lives. The other is to encourage you to explore and develop your own NSP, or *Normal Sense Perception.* Such an exploration will remove the incredulity which so often surrounds the prospect of considering and experiencing your own psychic abilities. Everyone has psychic abilities. Not everyone has explored some of the ways to develop them. . . .

NOW TO BEGIN . . .

The first step involves going inward to find a place which for you is experienced as an inner sanctuary, a retreat, or a place of inner peace. This is a real place in the inner environment of your mind and is to be explored with care, delight, and a sense of discovery. You will use the psychic abilities of seeing, hearing, and sensing as well as telepathic communication.

There is a distinction I want to make regarding your experience of *mental pictures.* These occur in two different modes which are important to understand. The two modes are *active imaging and receptive visualizing. Active imaging,* often called active imagination, is an intentionally created product of the conscious mind. This mode of expression has an electric or "moving-out quality" of energy which is aggressive in its nature and is very dynamic when intensely focused. Most cultures value the active, creative imagination because it helps one to be productive in the world. There is a doingness about it which we active Westerners like. Through active imaging we create buildings, transportation systems, educational processes, diagnostic techniques, and so on. Children as well as adults are usually highly praised for the fruits of their creative imaging.

Receptive visualizing, however, is a different experience which you have of the capacity to make mental pictures. It is the psychic ability called clairvoyance, in which pictures are *received* by the perceptual, subconscious part of the mind. There is a change in the quality of your mental energy in that it becomes magnetic or "drawing-in." This quality of receptive visualization occurs often in meditation when you have stilled the active part of your mind. I want to emphasize that this is not a passive state, as it may appear to be outwardly. Rather, it is a state of awareness which is *receptive* to whatever impressions, thoughts, pictures, or feelings may pass through it.

You probably have experiences with this receptive state of conscious without realizing it. When you were staring off into space without conscious thoughts, suddenly the picture of someone's face flashed before you. Perhaps in the wee hours of the morning when you have been in that half-waking, half-sleeping state you may have heard a voice say something to you, or heard some music coming from what seemed to be nowhere. You may have experienced a strong feeling that something was not going well for someone you were very close to. As an example of this later, or clairsentience experience, I will share with you something which recently happened to me.

A very close friend of mine had left for Europe for several months on business. One particular characteristic of this man which relates to this experience is the way he handles himself when he either is weary from a lot of traveling or confronted with a lot of chaotic disturbances around him. He withdraws into himself and just sort of disappears emotionally until he has sorted things out and is centered within himself again. For about two weeks after he had left I had not been in communication with him by mail. I awoke one morning with the strong feeling that he had totally disappeared from the face of the earth! I don't mean that he had died, just that he had withdrawn. So I opened my receptive channel and waited for impressions to come which would clarify the situation for me. I received pictures of him traveling a great deal, working hard, being surrounded by strangers most of the time and just simply becoming exhausted so that he had to withdraw to replenish his own energies. This withdrawal and my reception of it lasted for three and a half days. My experience was that I, too, was feeling weary, low on energy, and sensing chaos in my surroundings. However, when I looked at my own schedule, it simply did not warrant such a feeling. About the fourth day, my sense of withdrawnness totally lifted and, again, there was nothing within my daily events to explain what I had experienced. As it happened, a few days later I talked with my friend on the telephone and asked him what had been going on with him the previous week. He described exactly what I had seen and felt. It coincided with the days I had experienced it. We both laughed at this discovery and decided to use this openness to one another to explore some more areas psychically, inasmuch as there were some eight thousand miles of land between us. Over the next few weeks we each discovered many delightful new things and learned a great deal about our inner processes.

What I have just described was a personal psychic experience. To demonstrate that similar experiences are possible for you, I want to give you a very simple process to do. You can read the instructions and experience the visualization at the same time. Pause at the dots to clearly experience what is there with each step. If you like, you can have a friend read this process to you while you experience it. This is more effective because you can close your eyes and shut out all that your physical eyes usually observe.

Close your eyes and relax . . . See a familiar room which you are not now physically occupying . . . Be aware of all the textures, colors, and shapes . . . See each object within the room . . . Notice the placement of decorative items . . . Be aware of fragrances and odors . . . Listen to sounds inside or outside the room . . . When you have seen, heard, smelled, sensed all that you want to, return to your present location by opening your eyes or refocusing on the words on this page.

The experience you just had will give you an idea of how the mind receives a mental picture and all that is related to it. I didn't specify the room. Your mind received it. You were not physically in the room. You were mentally there.

Here is another process for you to do:

Close your eyes and relax . . . See, in your mind's eye, a supermarket . . . Enter it and go to the produce section . . . See a large bin of fresh, juicy oranges . . . Go over to it and select an orange which meets all of your qualifications . . . Pick it up and hold it in your hands . . . Feel the weight of it . . . Experience the texture of the rind . . . Smell the fragrance . . . Now, with your thumb break into the center of it and begin to peel the skin . . . Be aware of the effect of the citrus fragrance within your nose . . . When the skin is removed, feel the difference in texture of the orange . . . Again, with your thumb, break open the segments . . . Place a segment into your mouth and bite into it . . . Sense the juice flowing around in your mouth as it mixes with the saliva . . . Chew on the pulp . . . Feel the cool, refreshing juice slide down your throat . . . One by one, consume each of the sections, being aware of all of the sensations you experience . . . When the orange is gone go to the bin where there are some fresh lemons . . . Select one and take time to examine it as you did the orange . . . When you are ready, pick up a small knife nearby and cut the lemon open . . . Place a slice in your mouth and suck the juice from it . . . Be aware of the experience your mouth is having . . . Smell the lemon rind . . . Feel the juice slip down your throat . . . When you have had all that you want of the lemon, return from the experience simply by opening your eyes.

Again, this is a simple process whereby the mind enables you to experience many different things which are not in your actual physical environment. I have given you these two simple processes in order to prepare you for a more extensive inward journey. To fully realize this inner experience will require that you first use the active, creative part of your mind to follow my instructions. Then you will move to the receptive visualizing part of your mind and allow to come to you whatever is there to be received. Once you have received new information in this way you can move back into the active mode and evaluate whether or not and how you want to use the information. Become aware, as you undertake this journey, of the rhythm that is right for you in moving from one of the modes of your mind to the other. If I were sitting there with you, guiding your inward journey, I would sense the rhythm of your unfolding visions and go with it. For instance, when I take people through this process in my class, some go through it completely in about ten minutes while others take fifteen or twenty minutes. Since I am not sitting with you, the reader of this book, you will have to find your own sense of timing.

When you are ready to begin your journey, have someone read these instructions to you or read them and pause at each step to allow the visualization to present itself to you.

Close your eyes and relax . . . In your mind's eye see or sense yourself projected into a natural scene . . . See a place unfold before you, as if on a screen, a place which gives you a strong feeling of warm, uncomfortable, peaceful, relaxed safety . . . It might be a setting at the seashore, in the mountains, by a lake, in a meadow, etc. . . . Just get a sense of what the general area is like . . . Keep your eyes closed and take time to allow the details of this scene to pass through your mind . . . Allow your awareness to encompass the colors, textures, shapes, spaces, forms, sounds, and general ambience of your place . . . When you have noted the details of this inner sanctuary of the mind, get a sense of or begin to see a pathway emerging near where you are standing. Notice that off in the distance it blends with the scenery . . . Sense yourself walking along this path . . . As you look down the path or off in the distance you become aware of a radiant, blue-white glow which is moving slowly toward you . . . As you approach it, it gradually becomes transparent . . . Now the outline of a human form takes shape, although light continues to emanate from it . . . Slowly you see some garments covering the figure of this human-like form . . . As you and this figure come closer to each other, the details of the face, hair, eyes, bone structure and stature of this being become clearer . . . You now are aware as to whether this being is masculine in appearance and energy or feminine . . . In a warm, friendly manner this being approaches you . . . When you are quite close, you reach over and swiftly peel off the face as if it were a mask . . . Observe what is there . . . If, under the mask, there is a face which is frightening to you, step back and demand that the being leave your sanctuary, then mentally let go of it . . . Return to the path, walk along it and again see the radiant, blue-white glow beyond you. Slowly move toward it, repeating this part of the process . . . If, after the mask is peeled off, the face remains essentially the same, this being is your guide who now approaches you and placing an arm around your shoulder, leans close to your ear and whispers softly, "I am _____" . . . Now hear the name being spoken . . . Receive the first one that comes.

I would like to stop your inward journey here a moment and talk about what you may have experienced. I specifically did not do this to begin with as I didn't want you to have any expectations concerning what might happen. I wanted you to receive naturally whatever came. Now, let's look at what that may have been. First of all, if the sanctuary in which you found yourself seemed dark and formidable or even hostile, that could hardly be considered a place of peace, tranquility, and safety.

Go back and do the whole process again some other time when you are in a mood that is more positive and receptive. It's sort of like spooky places are out and safe, peaceful places are in. Okay? Now, what about the being or essence or personality or entity (whichever term you choose) who appeared out of the radiant glow? Well, if it seemed to be someone living whom you know, greet them as you would at any time and then let them go. This is not your spirit guide, which is the designation I give to that energy force field which you perceived on the path. If the being is in the physical body of a friend, they have all the limitations of the physical body, as do you, and so will be limited to their guidance, also. A true spirit guide has no such limitation.

What has happened is that this spirit guide, a nonphysical part of yourself but not a product of your imagination, is perceived by your receptive visualization as a form to which you can relate as you would to a friend. It is the expression of your higher consciousness, perceived as a form by the subconscious, psychic mind.

A Few Well-Chosen Words

O. M. Burke

Some people focus on an interest in psychic phenomena to the neglect of a more holistic approach to growth. A broader view of psychic matters sees them as events that may occur while on a deeper search for personal growth, but which can impede development if unduly emphasized. Patanjali, for example, who codified Indian yoga practices 1,500 years ago, listed a number of psychic phenomena (among them walking on water, clairvoyance) which occasionally emerged during the practice of yoga. At the end of this presentation of enticing potential powers, Patanjali says: "These are all barriers to spiritual growth."

In the selection that follows, a Sufi master addresses a group of persons who have sought his advice concerning psychic phenomena. The Sufis, a spiritual brotherhood whose members are largely in the Mideast and Asia, are known for their ability to develop psychic powers in a holistic framework.

Standing in the middle of his audience, the teacher immediately started to speak:

"Welcome. For as far back as there is any recorded history, people have been interested in two things: whether they would survive death, and seemingly occult phenomena. Students of humanity in every branch of science and scholastic discipline have tried to account for this interest. The method which most people seem to adopt in their search for the answers to the questions implicit in the two forms of interest to which I have referred has usually been the same. This method is to seek out things which seem to indicate the supernatural. Then the phenomena are studied and attempts are made to create or duplicate these phenomena. Alternatively, people who seem to control or to be controlled by their phenomena, to whatever degree, are sought and followed. One moment's thought, which few people will spare in their eagerness to find something out, would show the weakness of this method of approaching the supernatural phenomenon. I therefore invite you to ask yourselves, individually and collectively, what method you have established that you are competent to judge either theories or so-called proofs.

"This has never been established. The method which you are using is to try to understand something by means of something which is not objective: your ordinary, or even abnormal, mind.

"The Sufis in general will not discuss these matters with people who are not Sufis. The reason is that if they did, the non-Sufis would consider that they were mad; and the Sufis would be able to make no progress. Few people in their right minds would attempt to discuss, or evaluate, nuclear physics without preparation for the task. Yet almost every human being feels that he can have a reasonable opinion about the supernatural. He asks for information, it is true, for phenomena, for tales and demonstrations. But he does not ask for basic training to enable him to understand. This is like the child who goes to a school for the first time and expects to be taught a foreign language at an advanced level, without having any basic knowledge about that language, and what makes it up.

"The child is, not unnaturally, impatient. This is a characteristic of children. He sees people talking in a foreign language, and wants to know one, too. He sees the wonder, but not the mechanism. He asks questions which have no answers which he would understand, like: 'Who is the Moon?' or 'Why are two and two not three?' The child, however, can be told by the teacher or parent that 'It is so because it is so'; or 'This does not matter at the moment—eat up your food.' The 'raw' seeker after supernatural truth *can,* of course, be told these things by a teacher. But, unlike the ordinary infant, he will drift away from the stern 'parent' who talks like this. You can imagine the plight of the tiny infant who, instead of allowing the parent to discount his questionings, slips away and tries to live on his own: or seeks, every few days, another parent who will teach him the things he wants to know: not the things which he should be taught.''

The *Chutzpah* Factor in the Psychophysiology of Altered States of Consciousness

Kenneth Pelletier and Erik Peper

Biofeedback has been called the yoga of the West, because it combines Western hardware with Eastern techniques for altering states of consciousness. Pelletier and Peper, both young biofeedback researchers, present an account of remarkable phenomena and point to ways in which children might be trained to be masters of their bodies.

Biofeedback has been heralded as a quick path to the attainment of the higher states of consciousness exhibited by yogis and advanced meditators. In addition to this popular interest, meditation and biofeedback have emerged as a prominent area of research and clinical application in neurology, psychophysiology, and medicine, as well as the study of consciousness. Sophisticated instrumentation and computer analysis have enabled modern researchers to probe the nature of human consciousness with unprecedented accuracy.

Although the phenomenon of a marked degree of autonomic control has received much recent attention and has been recounted in anecdotes for hundreds of years, it also has been empirically verified since 1935

"The Chutzpah Factor in the Psychophysiology of Altered States of Consciousness" by Kenneth Pelletier and Erik Peper. Used with permission of the authors and the *Journal of Humanistic Psychology*.

when the French cardiologist Thérèse Brosse first recorded a marked degree of heart-rate control in yogis (Brosse, 1946). Since that time, there have been several major research projects which have reported marked degrees of brain wave, heart rate, and blood flow control. One of the most productive approaches to the study of altered states of consciousness and to the interaction between mind and body has been the intensive study of adept individuals.

Beginning in May 1971, Erik Peper heard about a visiting South American, a man who practiced unusual control over pain and bleeding, who walked on fire, had himself hoisted by hooks in the back, and regularly punctured his flesh without damage with sharpened bicycle spokes. We hoped that by taking physiological recordings from people who do these feats, we could convert this information to help the average person gain control over pain, bleeding, and other purportedly involuntary body functions.

Our intention has been to formulate a model of biofeedback and altered state phenomena which is comprehensive enough to encompass both subjective and physiological states. First, we approached the task of verifying whether or not these reported marked degrees of autonomic control were true. If true, the next issue was to have these adepts demonstrate their abilities under laboratory conditions in order to determine how they achieved this control. From this research, we hoped to create a biofeedback paradigm to teach others to attain comparable levels of autonomic control and psychological tranquility. It is important to note that each of these adepts maintains that they have no special ability and that anyone can attain an equal degree of autonomic autoregulation through concerted practice and meditation.

This first subject, a young Ecuadorian (R.C.T.), agreed on June 2, 1971, to spend a day and a half demonstrating his controls in a New York University laboratory. In an overcrowded EEG laboratory in the psychology department, while people churned around to gawk, Peper recorded the subject's EEG, heart rate, and GSR (galvanic skin response). R.C.T. proceeded to: chew and swallow pieces of an electric light bulb; to push sharpened bicycle spokes through one cheek, through the center of his mouth, and out through the other cheek . . . and push these spokes through the sides of his body while physiological parameters were measured. When R.C.T. pushed the unsterilized sharpened spokes through the skin, the presence of occipital alpha activity increased to 100% time in his EEG and the amplitude increased 73% over the eyes-closed baseline. This is unusual since normally we would expect alpha to block, which would indicate a stress response. Even though he has performed such punctures many times, he has few scars on his body.

According to such adepts, anyone can learn to control the pain and bleeding by quickly relaxing and then detaching their awareness (consciousness) away from the insertion point, since "pain is mainly the fear of pain and one's attention to pain." In R.C.T.'s case, he entered his meditative state rapidly and upon command, and this resulted in a rapid, unfocusing relaxation, and dissociation from any stimuli.

This experiment suggested that it may be possible to control pain by increasing alpha EEG. Based upon the research with R.C.T., a pilot study was conducted with two subjects who learned to increase their alpha with feedback as a means of pain control. One went to the dentist and kept her alpha on and therefore did not need novacain, while the other subject stuck safety pins through the back of his hand. The model would suggest that pain control seems to work if there is no alpha blockage.

Later in July 1972, with Marjorie and Herschel Toomim, Peper studied a 31-year-old karate expert, J.S.L., who placed a sharpened spoke through a fold in the skin of his forearm and suspended a 25-pound bucket of water from it.

The karate expert's occipital EEG consisted mainly of beta activity with some low-amplitude alpha; although the frontal leads showed some slowing, the main physiological change was an increase of the EKG from 81 to 100 beats when he stressed himself. He reported that instead of passively detaching his attention from his body, he focused upon a small point of energy which he subjectively moved upward from the bottom of his abdomen to a point where he inserted the needle. "Once you concentrate on that square, you can allow the energy to flow into any part of the body. The concentrated mind can be applied to anything it does, and when it is applied, it no longer feels. The concentrated mind is the activity itself; it does not exist in the world." Rather than a detachment of the experience, there was a total focus on sensation. This focus was associated with the absence of alpha, since alpha usually blocks when a person responds to stimulation. The common factor in the case of R.C.T. and the karate expert was the ability to maintain a fixed focus of attention. Whether the attention was focused away from or directly upon the puncture, the ability to control the pain remained the same.

Most recently, during August 1973, J.S. was tested by K. Pelletier in Dr. Joe Kamiya's Psychophysiology Laboratory at the Langley Porter

Neuropsychiatric Institute. In a week-long period of intensive research, J.S. pushed an unsterilized, sharpened knitting needle through his left bicep on three occasions while under the observation of an attending physician. . . . While he performed these punctures, he was being monitored on twelve psychophysiological channels which indicated [that he had] no response to the pain, and that he remained in a state of high alpha meditation before, during, and after the puncture. Previous bleeding: time tests had indicated that J.S. bled and responded to pain normally while out of his meditation state. J.S. was able to control completely the bleeding from those punctures and to heal the wounds within twenty-four hours without infection. (Similar findings have been reported about J.S. when he was tested in 1971 at the Menninger Foundation in Topeka, Kansas, and also with R.C.T.) When asked how he accomplished this control, he responded, "It's very simple. I do it by changing a single word. I don't stick a needle in *my* arm, I stick a needle through *an* arm. I move outside my body and look at the arm from a distance; with that detachment, it becomes an object. It is as though I am sticking the needle into the arm of a chair." This paradoxical degree of meditative awareness and detachment, often called "passive attention," has been observed to be a consistent characteristic of all of these adepts who are able to achieve a marked degree of autonomic control. Based upon this research, a clinical pilot study was performed with a patient suffering from pain due to multiple reconstructive surgeries on his face. Through alpha feedback the patient learned to progressively dissociate himself from the pain of a pin stuck in the back of his hand, and no alpha blocking was evidenced. This dissociation was successfully carried over into surgery. In many cases research with these adepts changed our belief structure of what is possible in self-control and self-healing and has helped to extend the parameters and possibilities of biofeedback training.

These demonstrations of autonomic control are important and impressive because they indicate that anyone can assert control over the healing process. The deeper meaning resides in the psychological state which permits such control to occur. All of these individuals have trained themselves to assume a particular transpersonal view of themselves which was summarized by Swami Rama as "all of the body is in the mind, but not all of the mind is in the body." This statement suggests that these individuals are able to enter into a meditative state of focused attention in which they are aware of but detached from their physical bodies. While such a concept appears alien to Western psychology, it has been an accepted aspect and goal of all Eastern meditative systems for centuries.

Implications of these meditative systems and our research indicates that individuals could be taught to control bleeding and pain in accidents, while undergoing surgery, or in a dentist's office. Also, this highly specific degree of control may be of use in such instances as cutting off blood flow to an inoperable tumor, correcting essential hypertension, or in the self-control over a migraine attack, headaches, epileptic seizures, or ulcers.

Based upon our research with adept individuals, both authors worked from the assumption that a very marked degree of autonomic control is possible. We have trained a number of subjects to attain voluntary control over electromyographic tension, peripheral temperature, galvanic skin response, and EEG with biofeedback.

An implicit assumption of our research is that any physiological function which can be monitored, amplified, and made visible or audible to the person can be brought under voluntary control. For example, some of our subjects have been able to increase their hand temperature as much as 18 °F, which means that there is a highly significant change in local blood blow. Similarly, subjects can be trained with feedback to control *single motor units.* This implies that with practice we can have voluntary control over single neuron firing. Thereby we have the ability to control our bodies to the micro level, again reinforcing our notion that we could heal ourselves through voluntary control. Possibly the localized control may explain the phenomenon of stigmata.

While some promising clinical work with biofeedback has been conducted with several of the disorders cited above, our research with individuals such as J.S., R.C.T., and J.S.L. has indicated that an even greater degree of self-initiated healing and personal growth is possible.

In studying these adepts, we have noted that physiological recording has been inadequate to assess some of the most important attributes of these remarkable individuals. Although the psychophysiological recordings, especially the EEG, have been of considerable importance in formulating biofeedback training paradigms, we feel that a considerable amount of information is deleted by focusing exclusively on the psychophysiology. In our experience, multivariate analytic techniques are necessary but not sufficient for explaining these phenomena. One of the most important factors excluded from a purely physiological analysis is how the control was initially developed and maintained. By studying the self-training procedure and the inner dynamics of these adepts, we hope to improve the range and technique of biofeedback training by focusing on the learning process. Without formal instruction, these adepts have learned to master their own fear. Often during childhood and early adolescence they created challenging situations for themselves with an attendant audience so that they had to perform or be seen as a "fool," since sticking needles in yourself is "obviously" a foolish act, but failing to do it after claiming it is even more foolish. By experiencing success in the mastery of these "foolish deeds," the adept learned "that the limit of their experience was the limit of their belief." This is the lesson which is taught by many meditative systems.

There are many disciplines, such as yoga, Zen, Tai Chi, judo, karate, which instruct individuals to overcome their own fear and obtain psychological and physiological mastery. In these various disciplines, the initiates are brought to the point where they must go beyond the teaching and incorporate the training in their own manner. Some individuals continue as perpetual students, others drop out, and a few succeed in true mastery.

Initial attainment of true mastery means going beyond what the individual initially thought was possible. Instead of looking at the precipice and retreating, the initiate must take the leap into the unknown. In many systems, the teacher pushes and allows no retreat by the student. This ability to transcend fear and enter into the unknown we have called the *"chutzpah* factor."* This *chutzpah* quality is most readily seen in our two subjects J.S. and R.C.T., since they developed themselves without the initial help of teachers or systems.

This process of self-discipline endowed them with an unusual degree of self-confidence and daring. Psychophysiological training and meditation were not the initial means by which they achieved voluntary control. These men taught themselves to achieve a remarkable degree of control and that ability was induced and sustained by this psychological quality of chutzpah. In our interviews, we noted that both of these men shared some common personality characteristics which appear to be elements of the chutzpah factor. One aspect of this factor is that they were rewarded in childhood for performing unusual feats such as R.C.T. hypnotizing his friends and then painlessly sewing buttons on their arms, or J.S.

---

*The *chutzpah* factor is a multidimensional parameter which has many interrelated factors and is best illustrated in the following example: At trial for murdering both his mother and father, the defendant pleaded for the mercy of the court because he was an orphan.

learning to lie upon a bed of nails with someone standing on his stomach. Under most conditions, such acts would be considered foolish or even destructive, but they are indicative of a unique state of self-awareness rather than simple antisocial acts.

Another important psychological factor which we have observed in these adepts is a willingness to accept what appears to be an impossible task or challenge. In fact, they appear to place themselves deliberately in demanding situations which will force them to perform a difficult task which they have never previously attempted. Most individuals avoid situations where failure may lead to physical or psychological injury. However, these adepts respond to challenges in a counter-phobic manner in the sense that they create situations in which the expectation of the people around them is sufficiently high that they are able to overcome their own fears and reservations. Hence, when R.C.T. claimed he could walk through fire (a wall of flames six feet wide and seven feet high) he did it before a live audience of 100 people and was shown on Channel 6 TV in Montreal on February 10, 1969. . . .

Lastly, another important psychological factor is the ability of these adepts to transcend social limitations and constraints. In terms of the Jungian types, the adepts appear to be extraverted intuitives who respond well to innovative and challenging situations. According to Jung, these individuals do not adhere to the socially accepted values and have a capacity to inspire and kindle enthusiasm for innovative views of social reality. Essentially, they are visionaries, and tend to express their vision in a convincing and charismatic manner. Since they have little patience for social convention or restraint, they may be unjustly condemned as insensitive or sensationalist, but this is mainly due to the fact that they value their conviction and unique view of reality above all else. They do not allow themselves to be constrained by the accepted limitations of social, physiological, or psychological standards, and thus they do not convince themselves that something is impossible before they have tried the task themselves. In essence, this quality of dramatic self-reliance accompanied by their own experience of themselves as capable of unusual tasks comprises the essence of the chutzpah factor. It is ironic that the educational system and childhood upbringing inhibits and punishes us for daring and chutzpah-inducing behavior, so that when a child has become an adult he has become afraid to try or afraid to "buck the system." Yet it is precisely these qualities, if maintained, which allow these adepts to achieve their self-mastery, a mastery which we now attempt to relearn by meditation and other forms of self-discipline.

Perhaps we could look at children and reward them for their daring, fearlessness, and for their "trouble making" instead of punishing them for the sake of conformity. In this manner we might reinforce the spirit of inquiry and self-assertiveness so that as adults they may not become helpless, hopeless victims, but responsible and competent for their own healing and growth process. It is our observation that patients who are trained (re-educated) with biofeedback not only learn control but also subtly change their attitudes and concepts which initially enhanced the disease process and take increased responsibility for their health.

Since this chutzpah factor has been developed to a pronounced degree in these adepts, there is a great deal which can be learned from their example. Their willingness to maintain an open mind concerning their fullest potential enables them to develop abilities which have been considered unlikely or impossible. An important factor in all systems of self-development and self-healing is the degree to which any individual believes in his ability to overcome obstacles of ill health or psychological distress. In research this is often dismissed or actively eliminated as experimental expectance, or placebo effects in clinical practice. All of the individuals discussed here, both adepts and patients, lend evidence to the power of volition and belief in the development of an individual's fullest potential. Today we are witnessing a remarkable convergence of ancient Eastern meditative systems and the most modern and sophisticated electronic instrumentations. Perhaps out of this interface there will emerge a Western yoga which will fulfill the arcane dictum of "know thyself." Above all else, the most striking aspect of this Western yoga is that it demonstrates that man has limited his growth through his own beliefs rather than through necessity. By daring to dream, imagine, and challenge these self-imposed limitations, man can learn to fulfill his human potential.

RELATED READING

T. BARBER et al., eds., *Biofeedback and Self-Control Reader,* 1970, 1971, 1972, Chicago: Aldine-Atherton, 1971, 1972, 1973.

BROSSE, THERESE, "A Psycho-Physiological Study," *Main Currents in Modern Thought,* 1946: 4, 77–84.

GREEN, E. E., A. M. GREEN, E. D. WALTERS, *A Demonstration of Voluntary Control of Bleeding and Pain.* Unpublished report, The Menninger Foundation, March 9, 1972.

KAMIYA, J., "Conscious Control of Brain Waves," *Psychology Today,* 1968:1, 57–60.

MULHOLLAND, T. B., "Biofeedback: It's Time to Try Hardware in the Classroom," *Psychology Today,* December 1973, 103–104.

PELLETIER, K. R., *Neurological, Psychophysiological, and Clinical Differentiation of the Alpha and Theta Altered States of Consciousness.* Unpublished Ph.D. dissertation, Psychology Clinic, University of California, Berkely, 1974.

PEPER, E., "Voluntary Pain Control: Physiological and Psychological Correlates," in *Alterations in Awareness and Human Potentialities,* ed. T. X. Barber. New York: Psychological Dimensions, Inc., 1974 (in press).

PEPER, E., *Biofeedback as a Core Technique in Clinical Therapies.* Paper presented at the American Psychological Association convention, Montreal, 1973.

Transpersonal Graduate Education

Robert Frager

Robert Frager is the director of the California Institute of Transpersonal Psychology, based in Palo Alto. It is probably the first program in the transpersonal domain to grant graduate degrees. The following brief selection is taken from the institute's brochure.

CURRICULUM

A graduate career devoted to purely intellectual development is no longer an adequate preparation for growth and research in psychology. The core of our program is the *balanced* development of the individual—the integration of the physical, emotional, intellectual, and spiritual aspects of the personality. Our goal is to explore and experience behavior in an environment that provides opportunities for intensive personal growth and integration.

"Transpersonal Graduate Education" by Robert Frager. From the brochure of the California Institute of Transpersonal Psychology that sets forth course offerings, faculty, etc. Used by permission of the author.

Five areas of study are emphasized. Each area involves intensive personal participation, academic study, and an emphasis on professional training related to therapy, counseling, teaching, and research. Tools for communication will be taught in each area.

1. Body Work

Students are expected to develop competence sufficient to teach a physical growth discipline or to practice professionally a body-oriented therapy. Body disciplines that will be available include:

Hatha Yoga	Alexander technique	Bioenergetics
T'ai-Chi	Feldenkrais method	Reichian therapy
Aikido	Dance and movement therapy	

Academic study includes course work in anatomy, physiology, nutrition, and kinesics. In addition to individual intensive training in a specific discipline, we provide basic familiarity with centering, relaxation, movement techniques, sexual therapy, and massage. We stress new ways of integrating various body disciplines and exploring how they complement one another.

2. Group Work

Extensive use of group techniques will allow students to work on communication skills and to develop a transpersonal orientation to group work, facilitating honesty, trust, and love. Instead of competition and grade-orientation we strongly emphasize the building of a sense of family, developing a supportive group community within the program. Specific systems include:

Gestalt Therapy	Rogerian group work
T.A.	Problem-oriented group work
Psychodrama	

3. Individual Work

Exposure to various techniques and systems of individual therapy and counseling will be available in order to facilitate personal development and clarification of individual goals, as well as for professional training. Systems offered include:

Psychoanalysis   Psychosynthesis
Jungian analysis   Client-centered therapy

4. Intellectual Work

At the core of the academic program is an in-depth study of a single system of philosophy or a single theorist in psychology, chosen by each student. General skills such as speed reading and memory training are offered. Students read what they are most interested in, teach each other what they have learned, and evaluate each other's work.

5. Spiritual Work

Emphasis is placed on a personal commitment to a specific path which will help to actualize each student's individual goals. We stress integration of one's spiritual discipline and perspective in daily life, along with periods of intensive retreat. The academic aspect will involve study of the Buddhist, Yogic, Jewish, and Christian traditions. Group meditation is a central part of the curriculum. Chanting, concentration exercises, and biofeedback training are also offered. We are working toward incorporating spiritual, transpersonal perspectives into all aspects of the program.

On Meditation

Wilson Van Dusen

Meditation is one of the foundations of transpersonal education. There are many ways to meditate—some easy, some more difficult. For example, most Zen masters advocate the cross-legged lotus position, which Westerners often find uncomfortable; on the other hand, Transcendental Meditation as taught by Maharishi Mahesh Yogi suggests that its practicioners sit in a comfortable chair. No matter what type of meditation is practiced, there are a number of observations that are commonly made as practice continues. Wilson Van Dusen, a psychologist who has been exploring inner spaces for many years, presents a concise summary of events that are likely to occur as persons explore their inner worlds through meditation.

Those who haven't spent hours meditating may well wonder why people bother. Those who have spent even twenty minutes a day meditating over a period of months are visibly different. They seem calmer, integrated, all together. It is as though they collected themselves and they remain collected. Their bodily movements are smoother, less hasty, more balanced. On inquiry they show considerable sensitivity, both inward and outward. Their knowledge of inner experience is noticeably beyond the average. Practice at stilling the mind lends peace to the individual. It also intensifies inner processes so that the individual can embark on a free self-analysis. It is a very intimate kind of learning because one isn't verbally talking about experiences but is working within experience itself. Also, stilling the mind gives one a refuge that can always be entered. I remember in one bitter life experience I was also meditating on the beauty of flames in the fireplace. Much of psychic disorder seems to stem from the psyche feeling it has no real alternatives. It must work out *this* problem, whatever it is. Meditation opens up alternate worlds as valid as that of one's painful problems.

Meditation is quite closely related to dealing with feeling-images. While heading in the same general direction as when working with feeling, it involves a greater focusing and limiting of the attention with a consequent increase in spontaneous inner processes. Meditation exposes more of the underlying nature of human experience itself.

The possible discoveries from meditation can be arranged in a rough series. Your first experiences are likely to illustrate how unruly the mind is. When you try to fix on a spot, all kinds of ideas may go through your head. You will find yourself asking, "Why am I doing this? When can I quit? I should be doing some work, etc." You will also discover a host of itches and intruding sensations. If you identify with the statements that call you away from meditation, you soon quit. Or you can let them go by like the comments of some impatient stranger. You don't have to identify with everything said in your head! The itches are a more fundamental resistance. If you don't scratch them, your first meditation can focus around the agonies of itching. Scratch the worst of them, but don't let the stubborn animal within get away with too much.

As you get into meditation, the mind, finding itself bereft of the usual garbage that occupies it, begins playing like a child. Your attention wanders from this to that aspect of the spot you are focused on. Gradually meanings are suggested. At this level you are close to what is experienced in feeling-images. For a long while the mind will skip around from an extraneous sound, to an itch, to implied meanings in the spot, to tiring of the eyes, etc. You may wrestle with the issues in this skipping around. You may wonder if you make the skipping. Generally the answer is no. As the restless mind tires of one aspect it lights on anything else handy. It is almost like an animal desperate to be occupied. If you look closely you may find it is almost impossible to trace the fading of interest in one thing before another replaces it. In fact, you may find you just went through a blankness only after you suddenly realize you are focused on a new aspect. There is a pattern: noticing one thing, fading interest, blankness, new interest emerging, sudden realization you lost the old focus. You may also flash back and forth between sensory or inward awareness and rediscovery of the spot. This is the beginning of a number of discoveries that suggest the operations of mind are much more spontaneous than we normally suspect.

There are a number of sensory changes that can emerge. You notice different aspects of the spot: it can move, become something not seen before, change color, and even disappear. This goes along with a successful focusing on a visual stimulus. Then it will vary the stimulus itself. These variations take on more and more dramatic meaning as though the spot were beginning to perform. It should take relatively little effort at this point to understand how the performance is related to your own life, for, after all, the performance is made out of your nature. If the performance gets lively enough you can even inwardly ask the spot questions and have it enact answers. At this point the results of meditation are rich enough to hold the attention to the spot.

Along the way a long battle may develop over how all this is controlled. You may wish to adopt one attitude and find its opposite reigning. You may want to keep the mind focused, yet it wanders so cleverly. You may even want to divest yourself of willfulness only to find you are being so willful about it. This is perhaps the most difficult rock and shoal of meditation. Things go much easier if you learn early that the inner processes have a will of their own and simply follow that will to learn from its direction. There are several alternatives in meditation if you have the problem of unwilling will. Don't identify with acts of will. For instance, if you find yourself saying, "I don't want to control this," don't identify with this willful statement. Even the effort not to will is willful. Willing, choosing, deciding, can be split away as autonomous processes that happen and drift by. Another way out is to exhaust the will. If willfulness can't be let go of, then use it ruthlessly until it is worn out. Some sail by the rocks of willfulness easily because they enjoy watching the inner drift of mind and never particularly want to control it.

There are also several pleasant plateaus of experience you can stumble upon. There is the discovery that meditation is a world of its own and that it can be returned to any time not only as a refuge, but to gain perspective on the outer world. In this state you may enjoy long periods of just feeling pleasant and peaceful. From this perspective thoughts of the outer world may seem rather distant and unreal. It is possible to review your behavior in that outer world and feel it was unnecessarily frantic or foolish. At this point the mind has become tame to the centering process itself. It no longer balks at focusing as it did at first. Related to this plateau are pleasant discoveries about time itself. The formerly inexorable clock-ticking time may languidly spread out and discover its own peace. Hours can become moments or moments hours. Time becomes stretchable and quite relative. Time itself may disappear as a useless issue.

After the mind is tamed to focus, it then playfully lays out a number of possibilities that gradually knit into a general understanding. Here the power of the inner message begins to carry over into your life. Life experience is not just another harsher world now; it is one of the components of meditation, the component in which you try out new insights.

The above experiences are sufficient reason for meditation. Yet within meditation it is possible to achieve a much higher state that has become the main goal for some. This has variously been called enlightenment, satori, moksha, and other terms. It comes at first as a very brief experience of seeing into the nature of things. At higher levels there are periods of a loss of self-identity and a sudden awareness of the total nature of creation. The higher levels of this experience are relatively rare. It would be well not to bend all one's efforts to attain this kind of breakthrough because effort certainly does delay its appearance. It would be wiser to enjoy and master all the lower levels of meditation first. Satori is more likely to occur where the individual has come to understand himself in depth. And this understanding of the self in depth is sufficient reason in itself for meditation.

A Basic Meditation

C. G. Hendricks
Russel Wills

Here is an easily learned form of meditation that can be used with students of all ages. This technique uses the natural ability of the mind to observe itself.

THOUGHT WATCHING

One of the most interesting worlds to explore is the world inside our heads. Something is always going on there, even when we're sleeping.

Although it is essential that we learn to observe our thought processes in our quest for self-understanding, we do not learn as much as we could for at least two reasons. First, it takes practice to learn to observe accurately, and we do not receive much encouragement for engaging in this type of activity. Second, we are too evaluative in our observations. No sooner do we see a thought of feeling than we rush to label it *good* or *bad, right,* or *wrong.*

One type of meditation, which originated in the Orient, involves just watching our thoughts in a nonevaluative way. The goal is to see the thoughts, images, and sounds as they are, without making judgments about them. And when we find ourselves making judgments about the thoughts, we try to observe those judgments.

This activity can be done by sitting or lying down.

Instructions

"Settle back and let your body relax, and as your body begins to quiet down and become comfortable, let your eyelids close. Relax a while in the darkness, letting your body become peaceful and comfortable. As you lie there, feel around until you find a place where you can find your pulse, and when you do, rest your fingers lightly on that place and get in touch with the quiet rhythm of your pulse as it moves the blood through your body."

Pause (thirty seconds)

"And now in the quiet, let's begin watching our thoughts and feelings that come through our minds . . . just looking and listening for the pictures and sounds in our heads. Pictures, voices, scenes, music, whatever comes in, just watch and listen . . . just observe. When you find yourself lost in thought, just return to watching and listening."

Pause (three to four minutes; work up to about ten minutes as the exercise is repeated).

"Now in the future, when you find yourself angry, sad, or bored, or in any kind of mood, happy or sad, just watch and listen to what is going on inside your head. This will help get you in touch with how you are feeling.

"Let yourself become alert at your own speed. Feel the alertness come into your body, stretching a little to feel more alert. Open your eyes and let the light in, feeling rested and calm."

Education and the Body

William C. Shutz

The body plays an important role in transpersonal education. Just as meditation, imagery, and dreamwork are ways of overcoming the conditioning placed upon the mind, there are many activities that can help the body overcome its history of negative conditioning. William Schutz, one of the pioneers of the human potential movement, presents an introduction to the role of the body.

THEORY OF PERSONALITY

Physiological aspect. The body is born with an inherited potential growth. Under optimal conditions all organs will grow to their capacity in size, function, and flexibility. Part of this growth—vegetative functions, emergency reactions, and so on—is determined by the lower centers of the brain, is primarily inherited, and only with great difficulty or

"Education and the Body" (editors' title) by William C. Shutz. From Raymond Corsini, ed., *Current Psychotherapies* (Itasca, Ill.: F. E. Peacock Publishers, Inc., 1973), pp. 408-11. Reproduced by permission of the publisher.

with esoteric methods (such as biofeedback) is subject to alteration by external factors. Another part of the growth of the body is determined by the higher brain centers, the cortex, and is subject to external factors including learning. Man differs from lower animals in the relatively small percentage of his capacity that is instinctive and the relatively large proportion that is subject to learning (Feldenkrais, 1972).

As a person develops, if his tissues and organs are all used in the various ways in which they are capable of being used, he develops to his full potential. Of course, no one does. Three factors prevent it: physical trauma, emotional trauma, and limited use.

To see how these factors inhibit growth, conceive of a person as a process rather than as a static entity. Most of the body is, in fact, in constant change. Except for the nervous system, all body cells are replaced approximately every two years. The person can be viewed as a process throughout time, starting at the moment the sperm enters the ovum. Seeing the person as a process can also be put in terms of constant transformations of energy, a concept that will prove valuable later.

As the body/person/process evolves through time, this optimal unfolding is altered by the three factors mentioned above. The distinction between natural or unimpeded evolution and optimal evolution is important. Unimpeded development, that is, development without trauma, will not lead to the body's development of all of its potential. The simple act of not impeding the child's sense of sound will not lead to his having a concert master's ear. His ear will be unflawed but not extraordinary. Similarly, growing up without being impeded does not guarantee full growth, as many classic studies of babies raised without sufficient handling have shown (Goldfarb, 1943).

As we view the body/person/process evolving through time, trauma and limits begin to affect body form, just as strong winds, fires, overcrowding, and periodic lack of nourishment affect the growth of a tree. And as with the tree the effect of these external factors can be read by observing the physical structure.

Physical trauma can interfere with the natural growth process (Rolf, 1972) just as constant external interference (pruning) reduces a full-grown tree to a midget bonsai. Suppose that a boy breaks an ankle early in life. During the healing process he feels unsteady on his feet and throws his weight forward onto his toes. This imbalance must be compensated for or else he will fall forward. The compensation may be accomplished by tightening the muscles in the small of the back. If these muscles become too strong, the body will fall backward so another compensation is made by thrusting the head forward. The resulting posture thus restores the feeling of body balance though at the cost of muscle tensions in the legs, back, and neck.

If this posture is adopted, through time, the muscle tensions become chronic and the muscle and connective tissue grow to hold these muscles in a rigid position. The muscles lose their ability to flex and relax as appropriate. Also, related structures are affected. The tight muscle, for example, may constrict a local blood vessel, partially closing it and restricting the blood supply to neighboring areas. Or the lungs may be prevented from inflating fully, thus cutting down on the oxygen supply. Or the spinal nerves issuing from the aberrated spine may be impinged upon and nerve impulses to the corresponding organs impaired. This can lead to a heightened susceptibility to disease of the affected organ. The area of impingement of nerves through misalignment of vertebrae (subluxations) is the subject matter of the field of chiropractic (Gallert, 1966).

Emotional trauma can also alter the course of physical development as has been shown especially in psychosomatics (Simeons, 1961) and bioenergetics (Lowen, 1971; W. Reich, 1949). The flow of the body/person/process is impeded by emotional trauma. Whenever a person has a feeling he wants to express and a conflicting feeling inhibits this expression, he is left with a tension in his body. This is particularly true if he is not aware of this conflict. If the same out-of-awareness conflict occurs frequently, the tense muscle will become chronic with the same result as described above. Take, for example, a person who when he was a child was never allowed to express his anger. When he got angry he wanted to bite, his eyes narrowed, his fists clenched, his shoulders drew back, his stomach tightened to prepare to strike, his stance widened to prepare for a counterblow. But his parents forbade the completion of these incipient actions. Soon the parents' prohibitions were internalized and whenever he felt anger he would inhibit himself. If this was a frequent occurrence, very likely his jaw muscle would become chronically tense, his eyes would form a permanent narrowing, his forearms would form a permanent narrowing, his forearms would be chronically tight, his shoulders held back, his stomach muscles would be very tense, and his stance would be a permanent straddle. The interdependence of the body organs is such that digestion, excretion, breathing, and so on are affected by these body changes. Certain illnesses, such as stomach trouble, now become more probable because of body tensions which weaken organs, making them more vulnerable to disease (Selye, 1950).

Limited use. The third limitation on the optimal unfolding of man is not as pathological as emotional trauma and may stem from social and psychological origins as well as from physical causes. Although our bodies are capable of moving in thousands of ways, as we grow up, a very small proportion of these ways is utilized. This applies to single movements, such as putting a leg over the head; and combinations of movements, such as the common game of rotating hand on stomach while patting the head. The number of combinations of things we can do simultaneously goes into the millions. Not using the body in all the ways it is capable of functioning leads to a restriction in movement and in intellectual, emotional, and sensation functioning (Feldenkrais, 1972). This is seen most clearly by observing people who do spend time developing an aspect of their potential to its fullest. An acrobat can move his pelvic muscles through a wide range of motion far beyond the ability of the normal person; the yogi has control of his breathing; the chess master has developed his analytical ability; the weight lifter his strength; and the piano tuner his sense of sound discrimination in ways that many normal people are capable of, but haven't done.

Lowen (1970) has stressed the intimate relationship between movement and other activities:

The functional identity of thinking and feeling stems from their common origin in body movement. Every movement of the body that is perceived by the conscious mind gives rise to both a feeling and a thought. The concept that body movements give rise to feelings and thoughts runs counter to ordinary thinking. . . . Seen from below, movement not only precedes but also provides the substance for our feelings and thoughts. We are accustomed to see movement as a result of thinking and feeling rather than the other way around. These informative movements are the involuntary bodily movements. Volitional movements, on the other hand, proceed from feeling and thought.

Lowen also makes the point similar to Feldenkrais', that movement is central to human functioning. "If thinking stems from movement, it follows that man's greater thinking capacity derives ultimately from the greater range of movements that he is capable of performing." (Lowen, 1970)

When learned movement uses a set of muscles in only one pattern it makes it more difficult for other patterns to be used with ease. An obvious example is the learning of a language. During this process the muscles of the mouth, tongue, vocal cords, neck, and the muscles used for breathing are trained in certain ways so as to make the appropriate sounds. The muscles accommodate to these positions so that making certain sounds in another language is very difficult to do since the musculature has been set. For a person with English as his native tongue this difficulty is especially evident when trying to pronounce German guttural or French nasal sounds. Thus to achieve the freedom to use alternate combinations of muscles often requires overcoming built-in resistances.

An unusually large number of simultaneous actions in a few brief seconds are performed by a professional quarterback. He must feel the football, turn it to the proper position for throwing, place his hand on it to throw, look for one or more receivers, step behind his blockers, move so as to avoid onrushing tacklers, fake a pass to one side of the field, look to the other, judge how hard and where to throw, decide whether to throw or run. Thus he must coordinate sight, sound, judgment, movement, effort, all at once. In ordinary life this kind of demand is rarely made.

In a series of ingenious exercises, Feldenkrais (1972) demonstrates how limited our body motions are and how restricted our capacities. At the same time he feels that these exercises demonstrate that by practicing unusual movements we send new messages to the nervous system that allow the nervous system to send new messages to the body to release some of the built-in restrictions and allow the body more freedom and mobility. Along with the new body freedom many subjects report a feeling of psychological loosening.

Here is an example of a Feldenkrais exercise (enormously condensed). Stand with your right arm extended straight out in front of you at shoulder level. Look at your hand and turn your arm, head, and eyes together to the right as far as they will go without strain. Note a point on the wall corresponding to that distance. Now come to the front position. Let your arm down. Relax. Put it up again to the front position. Move your arm to the right as before but simultaneously move your head to the left. Move both head and arm as far as you can go without strain. Do this five times, returning to the center position between trials. Be aware of the feelings in your neck, shoulders, and waist during these five movements. Put your arm down and relax. Now once again try the original motion of looking at your hand and moving your arm, head, and eyes to the right as far as they can go without strain. Compare it with the original point on the wall. Come back to the center position. Put your arm down and relax. Again put your arm in the front position. Now move your arm to the right and your head and hips (pelvis) to the left, all as far as they can go without strain. Do this five times, returning to the center position between trials. Again be very aware of all your body movements. Put your arm down and relax. Again try the original movement, moving to the right as far as you can go without strain. Compare this with the original points. It is probable that your arm now turns noticeably farther to the right than it did originally.

Now hold your left arm straight out to the front, look at your hand and turn your head, trunk, and arm to the left as far as you can without strain and note the point on the wall. Come back to the front. Put your arm down. Relax. Put it up again in the front position. Now *only in imagination* repeat the movement made for the right arm, three times each; that is, imagine your arm going left, and head going right, three times. Then imagine your arm going left and your head and hips going right three times. While you do this concentrate on the muscle feelings. After imagined movement open your eyes, and put your arm down and relax. Now put your left arm out in front as before, look at your hand, and move your arm, trunk, and head to the left and note the difference in the point on the wall. There will probably be about as large an increment as with the right side, although it was all done without movement.

Recent work on the Involuntary Nervous System provides an explanation for this ideational part of this exercise and for the body/mind view generally. Miller (1969) says:

Cellular electric current can be made to occur in protoplasm *by the very act of thinking. Thought alone* can therefore, in and of itself, be the *stimulus* to induce an electric current to flow down any nerve to the affected tissue—demonstrating that *thought is a source of energy.* . . . The Involuntary Nervous System is not necessarily involuntary . . . it is more under our conscious control than previously believed. (Italics in original.)

REFERENCES

FELDENKRAIS, M., *Awareness Through Movement.* New York: Harper & Row, 1972.

GOLDFARB, W., The Effects of Early Institutional Care on Adolescent Personality, *Journal of Experimental Education,* 1943, 12, 106-29.

GALLERT, M., *New Light on Therapeutic Energies.* London: Clark, 1966.

LOWEN, A., *Pleasure.* New York: Coward-McCann, 1970.

LOWEN, A., *The Language of the Body.* New York: Collier, 1971.

MILLER, H. B., "Emotions and Malignancy (hypnosis-psychiatry and organic tissue changes)." Paper presented at American Society of Clinical Hypnosis Convention, San Francisco, 1969.

REICH, W., *Character Analysis.* New York: Orgone Press, 1949.

ROLF, I., *Structural Integration*, in preparation.

SELYE, H., "Adaptive Responses to Stress," *Life Stress Bodily Diseases,* Association for Research of Nervous and Mental Disease, 1950, 29, 4.

SIMEONS, A. T. W., *Man's Presumptuous Brain.* New York: E. P. Dutton, 1961.

Why Johnny Can't Run

And Other Gym Class Scandals

George Leonard

George Leonard, author of Education and Ecstasy *and* The Ultimate Athlete, *is a sports fan of a very special sort. In this selection he explores some of the potentials of a new approach to physical education.*

One perfect spring morning in a small Virginia town, a group of thirty-five or forty boys and girls in their early teens were sitting on a grassy bank, attending to the instructions of a taut-muscled young man with gym shoes, gym pants, a white T-shirt, a crew cut, a whistle, and a clipboard. Next to the young man, like a guillotine in the sunlight, stood a chinning bar.

The man looked at his clipboard. "Babcock," he called.

There was a stir among the boys and girls. One of them rose and made his way to the chinning bar: Babcock, the classic fat boy.

Shoulders slumped, he stood beneath the bar. "I can't," he said.

"You can try," the man with the clipboard said.

"Why Johnny Can't Run" as it appeared in the August 1975 issue of *Atlantic Monthly*, pp. 54-60. From George Leonard, *The Ultimate Athlete* (New York: The Viking Press, Inc., 1975). Copyright© 1974, 1975 by George Leonard. All rights reserved. Reprinted by permission of The Viking Press, Inc. and The Sterling Lord Agency, Inc.

Babcock reached up with both hands, touched the bar limply—just that—and walked away, his eyes downcast, as all the boys and girls watched, seeming to share his shame and resignation.

This scene, which I happened upon a couple of years ago, contains no particularly noteworthy information. Yet it does evoke painful memories of an aspect of American schooling which many of us have managed to forget and which educational reformers have chosen, for the most part, to ignore. In an age when sports have become a major American spectacle, physical education in our schools remains mostly in the shadows. No significant national study has been conducted on the subject, which is considered a "frill" by some educational policy-makers, and even the most rudimentary facts and figures on the education of the body in this country are hard to come by.

In the elementary schools, where children are likely to form their basic physical self-image, offerings in physical education are very meager. The subject is typically taught, if it is taught at all, by classroom teachers who may or may not have had a course in "games and relays" during their teacher training. An especially enlightened school district might have one elementary physical education specialist shared among five to ten schools. Physical education in the formal sense is traditionally left to the secondary schools, and it is there that most of the painful memories accumulate. Indeed, a description of a traditional "P.E.," or "gym," class—the kind that still prevails in perhaps well over half of our junior high and high schools—tends to read like a caricature.

The class period begins with students scrambling to change into gym clothes, then standing for a quasi-military dress inspection. The military sensibility continues to hold sway through five or ten minutes of calisthenics—push-ups, sit-ups, jumping jacks, toe touches, knee bends. Students may then be ordered to run a lap around the track, though running laps is in some cases reserved by the instructor for use as a punishment. After this, discipline goes rather rapidly downhill as students move on to the game of the day—softball, volleyball, flag football, field hockey, basketball. Play is sometimes preceded by a brief status-confirmation ritual known as "choosing sides." What with all of this, there is little time for the game itself.

Students have yet one more ritual ahead of them: the shower. So much attention is devoted to this activity, in fact, that it might be seen by an anthropologist as the raison d'être of traditional physical education; in some schools students are inspected as they leave the shower room, ostensibly to make sure they are wet all over. Needless to say, boys' classes are separate from girls'.

Obviously this mode of instruction fails in its own proclaimed goal of significantly increasing physical fitness and skill. It offers too little sustained physical activity to increase heart-lung capacity. (This "training effect" is best achieved when an accelerated heart rate is maintained over an extended period—as in distance running, swimming, or cycling—while most team sports in gym classes are played in spurts.) It offers too little exercise, and often not the right kind, to build strength, flexibility, and agility. It offers too little individualized instruction to improve physical skills—balance, hand-eye coordination, fine muscle control—to any appreciable extent. And the activities it does offer are precisely those competitive team sports that the average person is least likely to play after school and college.

A few students in each class, already good at sports, excel in traditional P.E. and go on to a lifetime of rewarding physical activity. But many of the boys and a clear majority of the girls are simply confirmed in their ineptitude. Turned away from the potentialities of their own bodies, they smile approvingly at the familiar statement made by Dr. Robert Hutchins, among others: "Whenever I feel the urge to exercise coming on, I lie down until it passes over." A national survey by the President's Council on Physical Fitness and Sport in 1973 indicates that those who took physical education in school are more likely to exercise later in life than those who did not. But such "education" has hardly turned us into a physically aware nation. According to the survey (directed at adult physical fitness, not physical education in the schools), only 55 percent of adults report that they do any exercise at all. Of those who do, the majority name "walking" as their exercise. The favorite participatory sport of American adults is bowling, but nearly one half of the bowlers participate in their sport "less than once a month."

It is against this background that a major reform movement has at last begun to challenge the practices familiar to generations of P.E. students. "The New Physical Education," as it is called by the American Alliance for Health, Physical Education and Recreation (AAHPER), has by no means swept the field. It prevails in only one fourth of the nation's schools, according to the most optimistic estimate. It has not yet been examined by the national media. Many ranking educators have never heard of it, but it represents the viewpoint of most young teachers entering the field and is supported by such professional organizations as AAHPER, an affiliate of the National Education Association.

How can you recognize The New Physical Education? Literature distributed by AAPHER has characterized the reform in terms of "Lifetime Sports" rather than the usual team sports in secondary schools; "Movement Education" in elementary schools; and, in addition, individualized instruction and the inculcation of a "strong self-concept" all along the way. These general characterizations translate into changes that are fairly easy to spot. In junior high, high school, and even college classes, you might look first of all for a de-emphasis on dress code and showers and anything else that gets in the way of actual instruction and play. Then you will begin to notice the presence of such "recreational sports" as tennis, golf, and archery, along with sports that have not previously graced gymnasium floors. Students at San Rafael (California) High School, for example, can choose from an offering of forty-two sports, only a half-dozen of which could be called traditional team sports. Among the more exotic offerings are T'ai Chi Chuan, Body Conditioning, Yoga, Scuba Diving, and Rock Climbing.

"Some of these activities are very, very appealing to people who've been turned off by team sports," William H. Monti, a physical education reform leader at San Rafael High, explained. "A number of students who rebelled against all forms of physical education have gravitated toward rock climbing. These were the types who said they didn't like team sports of any kind. Later, of course, they found out that rock climbing involves as much teamwork as the traditional team sports, or more. They still love it.

"You know, rock climbing teaches the kind of thing we've always claimed for physical education—the ability to operate under stress. We create situations here in which stress is compounded by time. Running creates stress, but you can always stop if it gets too bad. During a rescue practice on a climb, when you have to tie a knot very quickly to take the pressure of a rope off your body, coolness and efficiency are absolutely required. And when you're tied to other people, teamwork and responsibility can mean life or death. In this sport, boys and girls and instructors work together and really *become* a team."

San Rafael, like other high schools with reformed programs, opens its sports activities to boys and girls alike. "When we first started modernizing our program about five years ago." Monti said, "we found that our women teachers had skills that men didn't have in some of these new areas, so we ended up with some women teaching all-boy classes. That didn't make much sense, so we started opening up all our classes to both sexes. At first, we even had girls playing touch football and basketball with boys. That was too much of a mismatch, but in almost everything else, we've found the mix is very good. We've found that co-ed classes in such things as volleyball and tennis push girls to improve much more rapidly than we though possible. We even have co-ed weight lifting classes. As you know, some experts believe that the large male-female difference in physical abilities is to a great extent due to cultural expectations, and that with the proper training, women can make tremendous strides in all sports.

"The main thing we're trying to do here is to help every student develop a good self-image. Body language is very important, and I think in physical education one's personal identity is realized more than in any other area of the curriculum. Students are different, and ideally, we'd like every student to have success in *some* area of physical education, and to *keep* having success. When enough successes have been deposited in a young person's bank account, then he or she can afford to take some risks in order to gain further success."

Along with a new emphasis on individual physical differences have come new and sophisticated methods for measuring and evaluating those differences. Missouri Western State College at St. Joseph, Missouri, for example, requires a "Concepts of Physical Activity" course for all students in general education. The course introduces the latest thinking on such matters as body type, fitness, nutrition, cardiovascular conditioning, posture, stress, and relaxation. But what makes it popular among students is that they themselves are the main subjects of study. During the semester, they go through a complete battery of physical tests.

First, they perform nine varied feats to discover their overall physical fitness. Skin folds at the chest, stomach, and tricep are then measured to estimate their percentages of body fat. Their silhouettes are projected on a screen so that their body types can be established. They do a five-minute step test to find out the heart's ability to return to normal pulse rate after exercise, run a measured twelve minutes to determine the body's capacity to process oxygen, and ride a bicycle ergometer to evaluate physical work capacity. Their isometric strength is measured by means of specially designed scales, and their isotonic strength by ability to do chins, dips, and jumps. Flexibility of the joints is measured. Posture is evaluated. Agility, reaction time, and speed are determined by timed tests. Finally, there is an evaluation of swimming ability.

Students at Missouri Western are not just tested and left with the evidence of their physical pluses and minuses, as is often the case with school testing programs; they are offered programs for improvement. The flexibility test, for instance, is followed by an introduction to flexibility exercises. At the end of the Concepts of Physical Activity course, students draw up their own physical summary profiles, which are compared to national norms. The profiles show where improvement is needed and also help in the choice of physical activities. Students are required, in fact, to write up a tentative personal physical activities program for both the college years and the adult years that follow. In this, they are guided by a long list of activities, some of which (aerobics, orienteering, tap dancing) would never appear in the Olympics.

"Seventy percent of body types are not represented at the Olympics," Dr. James Terry explained. Terry, an exercise physiologist, teaches the Concepts course at Missouri Western and runs the human performance lab there. "Highly competitive sports are appropriate only for a certain number of people. But there are sports or physical activities for every body type. There are good and poor activities for everybody. Maybe the person who is naturally heavy, the pure endomorph, shouldn't be a runner. But that person can swim, and swim more easily because of the higher percentage of body fat. The important thing is to get people started in *some* physical activity."

When Terry averaged out the fitness scores of the first 1000 persons he tested, he was appalled, "Most of our students are free from disease and physically unhealthy. That is, their general state of physical fitness is below the national college norm, which is pretty low anyway. More than 54 percent of all deaths in America last year were caused by disease of the heart of circulatory system. Medical doctors suspect that the stress and tensions of our way of life might be a major factor in the development of heart and blood vessel diseases." Terry, himself an avid jogger, sees exercise as a way toward relaxation as well as conditioning, and therefore as a key to good health. "We try to educate our students to the value of that vibrant, dynamic feeling that comes from being more than just well."

We have no way of knowing how much of our current sickness and malaise could be eliminated if people of all ages were turned on to "the vibrant, dynamic feeling that comes from being more than just well."

But a number of scientists, notably Dr. Rene Dubos, have marshaled evidence to show that way of life is a major factor in the incidence of sickness. The degenerative diseases—ulcers, colitis, asthma, arteriosclerosis, hypertension, obesity, and the like—are clearly assoicated with the lifestyle of the technologically advanced nations, and could undoubtedly be reduced by a change in that life-style, as could the current abuse of tobacco, alcohol, and other drugs. The healthy, fully active body provides the foundation for such a change.

In terms of health and economy, The New Physical Education makes good sense. What's more, professional journals, workshop sessions, and annual conventions of physical educators are filled with words of praise for it. Why, then, isn't it put into effect in every junior high, high school, and college in the nation? There are, of course, the usual inertia, the fear of change, the presence of an Old Guard too close to retirement for new-fangled ideas. But reformers in physical education face a problem unlike those of other educational reformers. It concerns their longtime love-hate relationship with athletics.

The male athletics department, which may or may not be part of the physical education department, is occupied with the voluntary, after-school, extramural sports program. Its job is to recruit, coach, and administer teams that will compete with teams in other schools. Athletics coaches are not necessarily members of the physical education department. The track coach might be a civics teacher. The football backfield coach might teach math. But athletics and physical education share common facilities; they use the same balls, the same gyms, the same fields. And, whenever possible, it is expected that physical educators will serve their stints as after-school coaches, for which they receive stipends from the athletics budget.

Actually, it's hard to draw a line between the two activities. And the athletics program, which serves relatively few students, often overshadows the physical education program, which serves all students. The backfield coach who is also a physical education teacher might support the theory of The New Physical Education, but he doesn't have time for it. He checks his sixty first-period students for proper dress, leads them through five minutes of calisthenics, gives them four volleyballs, and hurries back to continue analyzing the films of last week's football game with Central High.

In small communities with large high schols, the situation is particularly insusceptible to reform. There the high school football and basketball teams may well provide the town's major entertainment. Residents are proud to support their local athletics program while their own children go to seed physically. And those talented youngsters who do make the team may not be getting the best preparation for a long life of healthy play. This is especially true in the case of football, a vivid sport that can be hazardous to one's health.

"I view football as an act between consenting adults," Dr. George Sheehan said. Dr. Sheehan, a cardiologist and internist in Red Bank, New Jersey, is medical editor for *Runner's World* magazine and a leading authority on sports medicine. "Actually, football and baseball players are not in very good shape. The life expectancy of football players is significantly shorter than that of their classmates, and their tendency to become obese in later years is greater than usual."

Football players are strong, quick, and fast over a distance of forty to sixty yards. At any greater distance, they risk embarrassment. There is something preposterous about a strapping linebacker lying helplessly on the artificial turf being administered oxygen after an unexpected eighty-yard interception runback. Few indeed are the pro football players who can run a mile in four minutes and forty-seven seconds, which is what George Sheehan ran at age fifty in setting the world's record for that age and over. But you don't have to go to aging world's-record holders to illustrate the poor conditioning that prevails in this sport; literally thousands of amateur runners in their forties, fifties, and even sixties could beat the average pro player over the distance of a mile or longer. The glamour of competitive sports and the traditional dominance of athletics departments tend to blind us to facts such as these.

The demand for women's rights in sports and physical education, sharply focused by the provisions of Title IX of the Education Amendments Act of 1972, cuts two ways as far as reform is concerned. Title IX withholds federal funds from any school or college that discriminates on the basis of sex in any of its programs, including physical education and athletics. One can imagine the threat this law poses to athletic scholarship programs, which now favor the male sex. The law may tend to cool off the present hot chase for male athletic stars, encourage co-ed physical education, and aid the reform movement. On the other hand, it may simply encourage women to mimic the old male model, to go all out for scholarships in female competitive sports, and to end up with cries of "Winning isn't everything. It's the only thing."

Proponents of The New Physical Education are certainly not asking the athletics be done away with. They are asking for a balance between programs for the few and for the many. One reformer in a tightly knit community with a popular high school football team explained how this balance might be achieved. "Right now, we have an opening for a physical education teacher in our high school. We also need a backfield coach for the football team. In the old days, we would have recruited for a backfield coach, period. What we're doing now is interviewing people to find someone who is a physical educator first and a backfield coach second."

Changes in physical education in secondary school are needed, and they are possible, but the roots of change go down to the early elementary grades. There one may find a form of physical education that could revolutionize the way children feel about sports and their own bodies. It generally goes under the label of "Movement Education."

In the old-model physical education, children in the lower grades are likely to be playing games and relays. This means that a great deal of the time they are just standing or sitting around. In some games (dodge ball, for instance), they stand or sit around after being eliminated. In other games (kickball and other variations of baseball), they stand or sit around waiting for their turns to strike or catch the single ball that is shared by two whole teams. In still others (capture the flag), they stand or sit around in "jail" waiting to be rescued by a teammate. Almost always, they spend time milling about while the game or relay is being organized. And under these peculiar and inefficient circumstances, they are to learn whether they are "winners" or "losers."

It's just assumed, in this games-and-relays approach, that all children know how to move efficiently, to throw, to judge others' movements, to coordinate hand and eye. Of course this is not so. Many, perhaps most, first-graders are not very good at throwing or catching or performing other basic physical skills. Some children of that age, the majority of them boys, do happen to be good at the basic skills. Though the teacher may try to give all children a chance to play, the capable and aggressive boys tend to dominate the games. They become the "winners." And when the teacher is not supervising closely, these boys may begin forcing other children out of the games, helping establish that human category known as "losers." The girls drift away, realizing more and more that that athletic world is not for them. The unsuccessful boys find other things to do. Some of them retreat into books. Some become behavior problems. In the game itself voices become louder; movements become more frantic; play becomes rather unpleasant.

And the boys who dominate the games—the "winners"—are they getting the best physical education? Far from it. Driven to win, they are likely to repeat the primitive skills that first brought victory, and to compensate with aggression and large-muscle action for possible lack of the fine perceptions and small-muscle control required for high achievement in sports.

Movement Education, on the other hand, tries to cut the win/lose knot while systematically teaching the basic movement skills that are needed in sports and life. For one accustomed to the games-and-relays approach, a large room full of young children doing Movement Education makes a striking picture. In a class devoted to ball play, for example, every child has a ball and every child is moving.

"See if you can put the ball in the air without using your hands," the teacher says. The children use their feet, knees, forearms, wrists, elbows, and chins to handle the ball.

"Now roll your balls to each other, and see how many body parts you can use to stop them." More activity and experimentation. "Now, stand and move slowly around the room. Throw the balls to each other while you're moving. Throw gently." The air is filled with balls. Surprisingly, very few are dropped. Later, the children are asked to make up their own games with their balls. Everybody is involved.

The same approach is used for teaching balance, flexibility, strength, agility, control. Since the children are in constant motion, their acrobic capacity is also increased.

"The principles of the new approach to early physical education are simple," Dr. Margie Hanson, AAHPER elementary education consultant, told me. "There's a lot of equipment—every child has a ball or a jump rope. Every child is busy. No one gets eliminated. Everyone feels successful."

The equipment needed for Movement Education is not necessarily expensive. Most of it can be salvaged or built by teachers, parents, and children. For example, townspeople in Ocilla, Georgia, a village on the southern flatlands of that state, have worked together to create a model program in The New Physical Education. Large, brightly painted tractor tires provide a tricky environment for movement exploration. "Show me how you can move without bumping into anybody," a teacher says in a thick southern accent as children scramble over the tires. Other children walk the lines of a giant map of the United States painted on pavement, solving the problem of moving from Oregon to Florida without leaving a line and without running into anyone else. Young boys and girls learn hand-eye coordination with yarn balls and bean bags sewn by volunteers. Older children climb a stairway made of telephone-pole-sized posts of varied heights. Some walk on stilts made of empty coffee cans. Others make their way across balance beams built by amateur carpenters.

Once elementary school teachers become involved in Movement Education, they are likely to become its most enthusiastic advocates. But sometimes the demand for it comes first from parents who have seen demonstrations. Jack Capon, consultant in physical education for the Alameda Unified School District in California, is one of the specialists who travel around the country introducing people to the new approach. In addition to his crusading work in his own district, Capon gives up to fifty weekend workshops in other communities during a school year.

Capon believes that better development of perception and movement skills can improve a child's ability to read and write. But he views this possible improvement as a by-product. "If it were proved that our work also helped a child read, that would be a great bonus. But our goal should be primarily efficiency of movement. After all, what more fundamental right do we have than to move with comfort and control?"

Other educators and researchers are more insistent in arguing that there is a direct connection between ability to move and ability to learn. The argument gains force in the case of those learning disabilities that seem to appear so mysteriously in many of our children today. Seeking to explain the disabilities, the behaviorists point to deficiencies in the environment, to poor "contingencies of reinforcement." The psycho-analysts tend to attribute them to dark, quasi-sexual relationships in the family. Both of these explanations, though true as far as they go, seem to leave something out: the body itself, the way of moving, the way of *being* in the world.

One of the boldest theorists now linking movement with learning disabilities is Dr. A. Jean Ayres of the University of Southern California. Dr. Ayres has observed that vestiges of certain infant muscular reflexes tend to show up in children who have trouble learning. For example, when an infant's neck is turned to the right, its right arm tends to extend and its left arm to curl up around its head—a reflex motion that is self-protective. In the normal course of development, the reflex is "inte-grated" by nine months or so; in other words, the neck moves independently of the arms. In some children, however, this "tonic neck reflex" lingers on, so that there is unnecessary muscular action in the arms every time the head is turned. Sometimes the child will rotate the whole body to avoid rotation at the neck. Such an unwanted reflex makes graceful, controlled movements difficult. In addition, it can interfere with thinking. The reflex is normally integrated at the brainstem, so it is controlled automatically, without conscious thought. When it is not integrated, it must be controlled consciously, in the cortex of the brain, thus getting in the way of the child's attempt to read or to do other academic tasks.

The tonic neck reflex is only one of several for which Dr. Ayres has worked out a series of remedial physical activities. The Ayres work is usually offered not under the physical education program, but under the educationally handicapped program. Its primary aim is to improve not a child's ability to throw and catch a ball, but his ability to read and write. More and more studies show that the brain has something to do with perception and movement, that reading and writing are forms of perception and movement, that ultimately there is no way you can separate academic learning from movement, feeling, sensing, and the body.

I was greatly impressed when an Ayres-trained specialist unerringly picked out children with learning problems from random groups brought to her by their teachers, and did it with a series of simple movement tests taking no longer than five minutes. The specialist, Marsha Allen, a consultant to the Marin County (California) schools, was testing children in groups of eight and generally finding one or two children with infant reflexes in each group. Then a group came in that seemed to startle her.

She pulled the teacher to one side and said in a low voice: "I hope all your children aren't like these, because all of these are showing up with dysfunctions."

"Well no," the teacher answered. "They're not all like this. On an impulse—I don't know why—I brought you all my children with learning problems first."

The connection indeed seems clear. When our children are turned away from the joys of the body in motion, they are not merely losing their chance to compete someday in the Superstars; they are being deprived of what is fundamental to all learning—coordination, perception, health. Topflight competitive teams and television sports spectaculars are well and good; they inform us on the nature of human potential. But it would be ironic if the current sports boom ended up by making us even more passive spectators.

Transpersonal Communication in the Classroom

Barry K. Weinhold

Classrooms are places where people talk and listen to each other. That being the case, it's odd that schools require students to spend many years studying grammar, spelling, and other relatively trivial aspects of language but offer them little practice in communication skills.

Barry Weinhold has taught communication skills to children, parents, teachers, business people, and mental health professionals. Here he presents a concise summary of the hows and whys of good communication and problem-solving.

WHAT IS TRANSPERSONAL COMMUNICATION?

Transpersonal communication involves the use of skills and understanding to help individuals reach and maintain a conscious experience of their essential unity and connectedness with all life energy. It is based upon the belief that unity, not separateness or aloneness, is the basic human condition.

Transpersonal communication rests upon the foundation of effective interpersonal and intrapersonal means to bring people in contact with the highest in themselves and others. Effective interpersonal communication helps build an atmosphere of trust and connectedness with other people. Effective intrapersonal communication enables people to establish contact with and utilize their inner thoughts, feelings, and experiences. When people have this inner and outer trust and contact they are free to explore their beings at the highest levels.

Figure 1. Structure of Transpersonal Communication

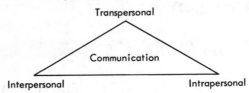

Transpersonal communication is designed to help people learn to trust the validity of their personal experiences and accept what they learn from these experiences as their best source of wisdom and truth. This includes both thinking and feeling processes. It teaches people to play hunches, use their intuition, and follow their thoughts and feelings rather than direct them in predetermined ways.

Trust in the validity of personal experiences will lead to an affirmation of the inner core of the person that transcends the cultural roles, ego defenses, muscular defenses, and emotional defenses (See Figure 2). This inner core is where unity with all life energy occurs.

All the numerous approaches to effective interpersonal and intrapersonal communications can be used creatively in this inner search for truth and meaning. Many of the methods developed for humanistic education can be utilized as a means toward these ends. Maslow (1971) proposed that education should help children to look within themselves and from this self-knowledge form their own values. Many humanistic educators stop short of this goal and maintain a more interpersonal focus to self-knowledge and value formation.

In summary, the main goal of transpersonal communication is the realization and maintenance of higher states of consciousness in which intrapersonal and interpersonal actualization is subsumed, not bypassed.

Figure 2. Levels of Self-Knowledge (Adapted from Lowen, *Bioenergetics*, 1975, p. 119)

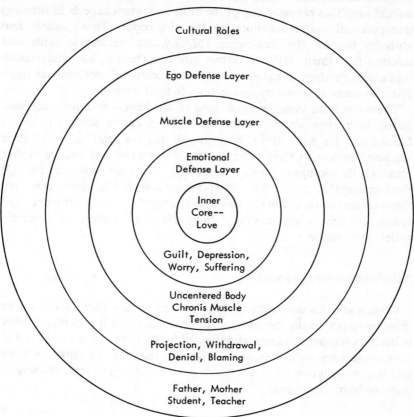

BELIEFS OF EFFECTIVE TEACHERS

Teachers who wish to develop transpersonal communication skills in themselves and their students need to examine their belief systems and attitudes toward teaching and learning. To be effective in fostering transpersonal communication in the classroom, a teacher must have faith in and commitment to the self-discovery process. This is a process whereby the teacher is able to create a learning environment that facilitates students in the development of their own self-knowledge.

Teachers teach more by *who they are* than by what they know. They model what they believe and they communicate their beliefs by what they do and say. This becomes one of the most important aspects of teaching transpersonal communications in the classroom. These beliefs and attitudes become the framework for any communication skills that teachers may learn. Without certain attitudes, beliefs, and understandings about children, the skills that teachers learn will not produce more effective transpersonal communications in their students.

There has been some research done on the beliefs and attitudes associated with effectiveness in teachers. An extensive study by Arthur Combs and his associates (1969) investigated the relationship of their teachers' beliefs to their effectiveness. They examined beliefs in five areas: (1) their subject or area of knowledge, (2) what people are like, (3) their concept of themselves, (4) purposes—society's, their own, and those related to their work, and (5) their approaches to their work. The results of this study suggested that effective teachers held certain beliefs in common.

Beliefs about area of knowledge.

Combs and his associates found that knowledge about subject area must be so personally meaningful to the teacher that it becomes a belief in itself. A teacher can *know* about individual differences in children, but if he doesn't *believe* it, he won't use it in his teaching. Teaching methods and the information related to them have to have personal meaning in order to be incorporated.

What are people like?

Here clear differences were found between effective and ineffective teachers.

Able—unable. Effective teachers perceive children as having the capacity to deal with their problems as opposed to doubting the capacity of children to solve problems.

Friendly—unfriendly. Effective teachers see children as being friendly and well-intentioned. They do not regard children as threatening and evil-intentioned.

Worthy—unworthy. Effective teachers see children as being worthy rather than unworthy. They see them as having dignity and integrity which must be respected and maintained. They do not see children as unimportant beings whose dignity and integrity may be violated or discounted.

Internally—externally motivated. Effective teachers see children's behavior as essentially coming from within rather than as a response to external stimuli, to be molded and directed. They see children as creative and dynamic rather than passive or static.

Dependable—undependable. Effective teachers see children as essentially trustworthy and dependable in the sense of behaving in predictable ways. They regard the behavior of children as understandable rather than capricious, unpredictable, or negative.

Helpful—hindering. Effective teachers see children as being basically willing to help. They regard children as important sources of satisfaction rather than as sources of frustration and suspicion.

WHAT AM I LIKE?

Effective teachers know how to use *self* as an instrument. They are willing and able to share themselves and to deal appropriately with themselves and life.

Identified—apart. Effective teachers feel identity with others rather than feeling apart from others. They see themselves as similar to others rather than removed, apart, or alienated from others.

Adequate—inadequate. Effective teachers feel basically adequate rather than inadequate, and capable of dealing with problems.

Trustworthy—untrustworthy. Effective teachers see themselves as essentially dependable and reliable. Ineffective teachers tend to have doubts about themselves in these areas.

Wanted—unwanted. Effective teachers see themselves as wanted rather than unwanted. They see themselves as essentially likeable, warm, attractive and responded to in this manner.

Worthy—unworthy. Effective teachers see themselves as worthy rather than unworthy. They see themselves as persons of dignity and integrity, worthy of respect.

What are my purposes?

The effective teachers were found to have goals different from those of ineffective teachers. The purposes of ineffective teachers tend to inhibit their ability to teach.

Freeing—controlling. Effective teachers see their purpose as that of freeing rather than of controlling people. They see the purpose of teaching as one of assisting, releasing, and facilitating rather than controlling, manipulating, coercing, blocking, or inhibiting behavior.

Larger issues—smaller ones. Effective teachers tend to be more concerned with large rather than small issues. They have a broad rather than narrow perspective. They seem to have more long-range than immediate and specific views.

Self-revealing—self-concealing. Effective teachers are more likely to be self-revealing than self-concealing. They are willing to disclose the self and can treat their feelings and shortcomings as important and be open about them. They seem willing to be persons and not roles.

Involved—alienated. Effective teachers tend to be involved with people rather than alienated from them. Their purpose is to enter into interaction with students rather than being inert or remaining aloof or remote.

Process-oriented—goal-oriented. Effective teachers are more interested in processes than achieving goals. They see their purpose as that of encouraging and facilitating the process of search and discovery as opposed to working toward some personal goal or preconceived solution.

Approaches to the task

Teachers' beliefs about how to approach the teaching-learning task were found to relate to their success in carrying out the task.

People—things.   Effective teachers are more oriented toward people than things. They have a student rather than a subject orientation.

Subjective—objective.   Effective teachers are more likely to approach students subjectively and are more concerned with the learning experience rather than teaching objective facts.

TEACHERS' MISCONCEPTIONS ABOUT CHILDREN

Teachers often don't understand children because they see them as miniature adults and want them to behave like adults. When children behave like children instead of adults, often teachers feel angry, scared, and sad. Admittedly, it would be easier to teach if children looked at the world and behaved as adults do. However, they don't; understanding how they look at the world and why they do and say what they do helps to build the rapport needed for effective teaching (Holt, 1974). Below are some characteristics teachers tend to overlook:

1. Children are concrete and not abstract. They need concrete examples in order to understand concepts.
2. They seem happy and carefree because they use their energy and curiosity to discover new things and not to brood about old things.
3. Even though they seem happy and carefree they have as many fears as most adults.
4. They are very sensual. They are tuned into their senses and respond to what their senses tell them. They often do what feels good at the moment.
5. They are very self-absorbed and self-centered. They don't naturally see things from another person's point of view. This quality needs to be developed through interaction with other children.
6. They often appear cruel and inconsiderate. What adults fail to see is that whether they are cruel or kind depends upon an impulse rather than a plan or principle.

ELEMENTS OF EFFECTIVE TEACHER-STUDENT RELATIONSHIPS

In order to build an effective relationship with students, a teacher must be able to see children the way they are and not the way adults would like children to be. In addition, teachers and students need the following:

1. *Openness*—Each must be willing to risk being open, direct, and honest with the other.
2. *Caring*—Each must value the relationship and care what happens to the other.
3. *Interdependence* (as opposed to dependence)—Each must view his goals as characterized by interrelatedness.
4. *Separateness*—Each must be willing to see the other as a separate person who will grow and develop in unique, creative, and individual ways.
5. *Mutual needs and wants*—Neither person's needs and wants can be met at the expense of the other's.

POWER AND AUTHORITY

Children are attracted by the natural authority of any adult who responds authentically and respectfully to them. Many teachers are confused about their power and authority and give double messages to children. Natural authority or power is based upon expertise, knowledge, experience, and a willingness to treat others who may have fewer of these qualities with respect and genuineness.

Teachers who are afraid of losing their authority or power are concerned about another kind of power: the power to give rewards and punishments. This power works only as long as those receiving the rewards and punishments are dependent on them or at least think they are. As students become more mature psychologically and adopt a more internal frame of reference, they have less need for this kind of authority.

The need to relate to other people from an authentic and respectful position does not decrease. The process whereby students can move toward an interpersonal framework requires this kind of nurturing, supportive, freeing authority.

Rollo May (1972) defines power as the ability to cause or prevent change. He sees five types of power present in every person all the time and holds that each person must learn to use the kind of power appropriate to a particular situation. The five types of power are: (1) *exploitative,* where the strong meet their needs at the expense of the weak; (2) *manipulative,* where the strong collude to get the weak to cooperate so the strong can get their needs met; (3) *competitive,* where the strong use their power to defeat another strong person (this is the only kind of power with both destructive and creative forces); (4) *nurturant,* where the strong use their power for the benefit of others; (5) *integrative,* where the strong use their power with another to benefit both.

Natural power in people is the *power to be*. The use of integrative power recognizes the *power to be* as natural and part of the transpersonal unity all people share. Teachers who utilize integrative power with their students are affirming the *power to be* necessary for effective transpersonal communication.

INTERPERSONAL COMMUNICATION

Effective interpersonal communication is a necessary part of developing a framework for transpersonal communication. Below is a list of basic concepts for effective interpersonal communication in the classroom:

1. What people behave upon is their *perception* of what others have said or done, not what really has been said or done.
2. People need skills to help them check their perceptions against reality.
3. People can think and feel at the same time and need to use both thinking and feeling in solving problems.
4. There is no such thing as a "bad feeling." Feelings are natural and important cues telling people they need and/or want something.
5. Needs are things that only one person can meet.
6. Wants are things that you can get from a number of people.

There is a healthy way of processing feelings and using energy that comes from feelings to get wants and needs met (Falzett and Maxwell, 1974).

HEALTHY BEHAVIORAL PROGRESSION

1. Person becomes aware of an unmet need/want which leads to
2. feelings (sad, scared, angry) which if the person has permission to feel them will lead to
3. thoughts about the need or want and related needs and wants and
4. how these are connected to significant persons in the environment and to this specific situation which leads to
5. the person generating options for getting the need or want met which leads to
6. a decision to act on one of the options which
7. turns the feelings of fear, sadness, or anger into excitement which, if the option leads to the person getting what he needed, turns to feelings of happiness/joy.

HEALTHY FEELING STRUCTURE

The basic structure for communicating feelings/wants is:

"I am _____
        [feeling: sad/scared/angry]

about _____
        [situation/person's behavior]

and I want from you _____
Are you willing to give me that?"

Many people need permission and support in order to deal effectively with their feelings. One of the most helpful ways to deal with feelings is to listen to them and respond in a listening manner. Example: "You seem *(feeling word)* about *(facts)."* This allows the other person to "own" his feelings and begin to use them to solve problems. Students in your classroom will need to learn effective ways to deal with and use their feelings to get needs and wants met. What follows are some definitions of some basic feelings and suggestions on how to deal effectively with students having these feelings.

HOW TO DEAL WITH HEALTHY FEELINGS IN OTHERS

Feelings	Definition	Suggestion on What to Say
1. Angry	A response to not getting a want/need met. May not have permission to express anger and is scared, too.	"Wow, you are really angry about something, do you want to talk about it?"
2. Scared	Person perceives physical or emotional danger. May not have permission to think and feel at the same time. May be covering anger.	"You look afraid of something. Do you want to talk about it with me?" "You can be scared and still think about what you want/need." "The scared feeling's telling you to think of something that would make things better."
3. Sad	About the loss of a person, thing, or relationship (real or fantasy). It is an important part of "giving up" something you are attached to. There may be some anger connected with the loss.	"You are looking sad today. Will you talk to me about it?" "It's ok to feel sad about that." "Cry about it if you need to." "It's ok to be mad, too, about losing that."

Feelings	*Definition*	*Suggestion on What to Say*
4. Excited	Anticipation of something good happening. Scared and excited are closely related. Some children don't have permission to show excitement.	"You are really excited about your birthday party." [situation] "It's ok to feel good about the plans you have made."
5. Happy or Joyful	Satisfaction is getting what you wanted/needed, or doing something effectively. Some people don't know it's acceptable to be effective and be happy.	"You look really pleased about the story you wrote." "It's really neat that you took care of yourself by asking for what you want."

Some people use other words as feelings and these often become ways to avoid the basic feeling or to justify behavior. Words like "frustrated," "guilty," "hurt," "annoyed," or "irritated" are usually covering anger. Words like "confused," "nervous," "uneasy," or "tense" cover scared. Sadness is often expressed as "lonely," "bored," "empty," or "low." Some words represent a combination of feelings. "Depressed," "unhappy," or "upset" can be a combination of anger, fear, and/or sadness. Suffering is usually anger and fear operating in a person who doesn't have permission to express these emotions.

HOW TO TEACH EFFECTIVE THINKING AND PROBLEM SOLVING

Many children come to school having already decided not to think effectively and not to solve problems. The way that teachers relate to them will either reinforce that decision or help them redecide. Many of the thinking problems in school-age children are the result of adaptive patterns in which they have gotten their parents or other adults to do their thinking and problem solving for them (unhealthy symbiosis). This is a natural occurrence in children before the age of two, but if parents don't begin to transfer the thinking and problem-solving responsibility, children don't learn to think and take care of themselves in appropriate ways (Schiff & Schiff, 1971). Teaching children to think and solve problems then becomes an important task of the teacher. This is part of the process of teaching responsibility (response-ability) or the ability to think and respond appropriately in a situation. Being responsible therefore means doing or saying what you already know is appropriate to do in a situation.

Children use passivity and discounting to avoid thinking and solving problems for themselves. If teachers recognize these avoidance techniques, they will be able to confront them effectively and help children decide to stop using them.

PASSIVE BEHAVIORS AND HOW TO CONFRONT THEM EFFECTIVELY

Behavior	Reasons for the Behavior	What to Say and Do
1. Does nothing. May say "I don't know" a lot when faced with a problem. Shy children may do this frequently. May not answer questions. May engage in long silences before answering simple questions.	Hopes that you will do the thinking. Learned that appearing weak and helpless got someone else to think for them.	"I know you have that information, so how about your thinking about it and letting me know when you have." "I expect you to think." "If you need information that you don't have, you can ask for it." "Think about what you need from me (or others) and ask for it."
2. Overadaptation.	People in this position don't learn reasons for things. Usually have faulty cause and effect relationships. This leaves the responsibility with another person to solve the problem.	"What are your reasons for doing that?" "People have reasons for doing what they do and I expect you to think about what you want to do and why you want to do it." Need to make sure the person sets his own goals that take into account (1) what is appropriate for the situation (2) his feelings, and (3) other people's feelings.
3. Agitation. These are nonproductive repetitive behaviors (tapping a pencil, chewing on an eraser, pacing back and forth, talking without saying anything new).	They are attempts to avoid solving a problem by waiting out someone or making them uncomfortable enough so they solve the problem instead.	"Stop that and think about what you want." "Instead of doing that, I want you to put energy into solving the problem."
4. Incapacitation or violence. These include temper tantrums—kicking, hitting, breaking something or hitting someone, or developing physical symptoms—fainting, having a seizure, etc.	This is a more desperate attempt to get someone to take responsibility. Following the discharge of energy is a good time to give them messages to think and solve problems more effectively.	Take whatever steps necessary to restore order or control. The person is out of control and at that point taking control is appropriate. Following the blowup: "It is not ok for you to solve problems that way." "Think about what you could have done instead to solve problems."

DISCOUNTING

Instead of solving problems, people often suffer about them and engage in discounts about the problem. They may pretend that there isn't a problem and block their feelings. To do that they may get giddy, depressed, or engage in repetitive behavior to avoid thinking/feeling about it. They may deny the significance of a problem and may attempt to block feelings. They may say that they are not angry/scared/sad/excited enough to do anything about their feelings. They may act as if there is nothing that can be done about the problem. Finally, they discount their ability to deal with problems. Discounts need to be confronted with caring to get people to stop suffering and get them to deal with what is bothering them.

HOW TO DEAL WITH DISCOUNTS

Discount	*Confrontation*
1. "There's nothing the matter." (Problem discount)	"How about your thinking about what you are feeling?" "I'm willing to talk to you about it if you want to." "It is not ok with me for you to discount your feelings. They are important and you can deal with your feelings or ask for help."
2. "Oh, it's not important; I'll probably feel better tomorrow." (Significance discount)	"Sounds like you are having some feelings that you are not dealing with." "Will you think about what you are feeling and talk to me about it?" "It's not ok with me for you to discount the importance of your feelings."
3. "Well, there is nothing that can be done anyway." (Solvability discount)	"Sounds like it seems hopeless to you right now." "Will you think about what you are willing to do about your problem? Only if you have tried at least ten options without success will I accept your definition that it is hopeless." "You can think effectively and solve problems."
4. "I don't know what to do, it's too much to think about." (Self-discount)	"Sounds like you are feeling helpless about solving your problem." "You can think and feel at the same time and use both to solve your problem." "How about thinking about what you can do to solve the problem."

Many students will not learn to think and solve problems unless you are willing to put energy into confronting passivity and discounting. Since the way out of passivity is for the passive person to think about what he wants or needs and how to get it, he must be willing to stop using passivity and discounting to get what he wants. You also need to make sure that you don't support any of the passive behaviors. One of the most common ways that teachers support passivity is through Rescuing. Rescuing is defined as doing something for someone else that she/he could do for himself/herself. Common forms of Rescuing involve thinking and solving problems for a passive person who could do that for himself/herself. Teachers who engage in Rescuing use it to achieve feelings of being needed and important, control over another person, and avoidance of problems in themselves.

PERMISSIONS

Another effective way to promote healthy interpersonal and intrapersonal communication is through the use of permissions. Many students at some time in their past have been given negative messages (verbal or nonverbal, direct or indirect) about their abilities or their personal worth. These children need to receive permissions or positive messages from teachers and others to replace the negative ones. The negative messages are often in the form of injunctions (Don't think, Don't be you, etc.) or attributions (Be lazy, Be a child, Be passive). Permissions are "You can" or "I expect you to" statements. If the teacher has established rapport with a student, then permissions may be an extremely helpful way to promote effective behavior. The negative messages are often tied to passivity and discounting and support "not ok" decisions the person has made. Below are listed some commonly held injunctions with the appropriate permission statement for each.

HOW TO GIVE PERMISSIONS

Negative Message	Permission
1. "Don't have needs and wants of your own."	"You can figure out what you want for yourself from this class and decide how to get it."
2. "Don't think."	"I expect you to think about what you want and take care of yourself by asking for what you want."
3. "Don't be you."	"It's ok to be you and get what you want."
4. "Don't feel (angry, sad)."	"It's ok to feel angry and decide how to express it appropriately."
5. "Don't question things, just do them."	"It's ok to question why rules are made and to think of reasons for doing things."

Since thinking, feeling, problem solving, and active meeting of one's needs and wants are necessary to breaking the unhealthy symbiosis, permissions in these areas are particularly useful. Permissions that many children need to hear are that they are expected to think, to ask for what they need and want, and that it's ok for them to grow up. An indirect way to give a child permission to think is to say to a child who asks you to solve a problem for him: "How about you figuring out what to do about that and coming to talk to me when you have figured it out." Even if the child is unable to figure it out, you have given him permission to think and then ask for information that he needs to figure it out.

THINK STRUCTURES AND PROBLEM-SOLVING STRUCTURES

There are a number of ways to teach students how to mobilize their thinking processes and how to solve problems effectively. Again, the most effective way is to model the behavioral skills that you wish your students to learn.

Levin (1973) developed a simple way for teaching effective thinking that is presented in modified form below:

I am _____ *and I think (or fantasize)*
            [feeling word]
that if I _____
                 [what behavior]
I will be _____
                   [what others will do to you]
instead of _____
                     [what you would like others to do]
so I _____
              [what you usually do: a game, passivity or discounting]

After you ask someone to diagram this negative think structure, ask him to think about what he could do to get the response he wants.

Problem solving from a position of equal power and equal responsibility is necessary to promote effective interpersonal communication in the classroom (Gordon, 1974). The process presumes that students and teachers are convinced that a win-win structure is possible and the other skills are operating at a high level.

The six steps in problem solving are listed below:

Step One—Defining the Problem. Each person has a turn stating what he thinks the problem is and how he feels about it. The other person listens and restates what he/she heard the other say and checks out whether or not that is what was meant (negotiation for meaning). Then both state and agree on a definition of the problem. State the problem in terms of unmet needs and wants and not solutions. Example: "I cannot hear the group I am working with and I'm angry about that" instead of "I want it quiet in this room" (solution).

Step Two—Brainstorming Possible Solutions.   All ideas or possible solutions are accepted without evaluation. What do you need/want and what does the other person need/want to feel good about himself or the problem?

Step Three—Evaluating the Possible Solutions.   Estimate what the probabilities of success are for each possible solution and consider what internal and external resources are necessary and available to make the solution work. Ask: "How can each of us get as much as possible of what we want?"

Step Four—Deciding Upon a Solution.   "Which solution would I feel best about?" Agree on the one that "feels best" to both of you and write down what is expected by both parties.

Step Five—Implementing the Solution.   Determine who is to do what by when. Be specific about this and write it into the contract, including a deadline for implementing the solution.

Step Six—Evaluating the Success of the Solution.   It is also important to agree that if for some reason the solution no longer is working for one of the parties, he/she can request another problem-solving session and the process will begin all over again. Therefore, the contract is always open-ended.

CONTRACTS

Contracts can be an effective tool for developing good interpersonal communication in the classroom because (1) they spell out rules and policies, (2) they make expectations clear, (3) they allow students to question and understand rules and expectations, (4) they set up a structure in which there is mutual responsibility for enforcing the conditions of the contract.

One form of contract used by some teachers is a no-discount contract. In this, two or more people have an agreement not to discount themselves or each other. This kind of contract can become the framework for effective thinking. If the student contracts to say what he doesn't like and what he wants to do instead, he really has to think about how to structure time for himself.

A no-discount contract may look like the following:

Because we work together and both have needs and wants to be successful, we agree that we will not intentionally discount ourselves, the other person, or the importance and solvability of problems. We agree to state what we don't like and what we want instead. We agree to confront any unintentional discounts that we perceive in ourselves or the other person. We agree to say what we don't like in a way that doesn't put the other person down. We agree to solve all problems that arise in the classroom (or outside, if they affect us) so we both get our needs/ wants met.

This contract is our way of agreeing to work together, cooperate, and assume equal responsibility for making this classroom a place where we both want to be and feel good.

Signed: _____
[teacher]

_____
[student or students]

Other similar contracts can be used for schoolwork. Also, cooperative rule setting for the classroom can be developed and stated in contract form.

COMMON ERRORS IN INTERPERSONAL COMMUNICATION

Below is a list of the common errors people make in communicating with other people.

1. Making a statement instead of asking for what you want or need: "I wish you were going into town."
2. Asking a question instead of making a statement: "Don't you think that. . .?"
3. Saying "I feel" to mean "I think": "I feel that you are rude."
4. Saying "one" or "people" or "you" in expressing your point of view: "People are afraid to. . ."
5. In a group, talking about a person and not to him or her: "I like her idea."
6. Using "I can't" to mean "I don't" or "I don't want to": "I can't go with you because I'm too tired."

7. Using "have to's" and "shoulds" when you mean "choose to": "I have to go to the school play tonight."
8. Not answering a question directly: "How do you feel today?" "Why do you want to know?"
9. Using words like "I guess," "I think," "maybe," when you are sure.
10. Using "try" instead of "do": "I'll try to do that today" instead of "I'll do that today."
11. Blaming your feelings on someone else: "You made me angry" instead of "I am angry."
12. Confusing inference and observation: "John is a poor sport" instead of "John hit Jimmy with the ball and [observation] I think he is a poor sport [inference]."
13. Interrupting someone when he is speaking. This usually means you aren't listening.
14. Changing the subject, or "chaining." This is listening to just enough of what someone says to change the subject to something you know more about or want to talk about. First person: "I watched the Monday night football game and it was really exciting." Response: "We have tickets to see the Colorado-Nebraska football game next week."
15. Using statements like "always" or "never" to support your point of view.

INTRAPERSONAL COMMUNICATION

The ability of a person to stay in touch with what is happening inside of him is referred to as intrapersonal communication. Another way to express this is self-awareness: how aware you are of what is going on inside of you, outside of you, and how you are relating these experiences to yourself, as opposed to relating them to others (interpersonal).

ESSENTIAL INTRAPERSONAL PROCESSES

Intrapersonal communication can be thought of in several ways:

1. Awareness of what is going on inside of you. This would include awareness of the signals your body is sending out all the time: the tensions you feel in your muscles; the physical sensations that go with feelings; and feelings themselves. It also includes awareness of the inner world of thoughts and ideas.
2. Awareness of what is happening around you. This includes what your senses tell you about what is present in the here and now.

3. Awareness of past events and how these events influence you in the present. Sometimes past events continue to influence us in ways of which we are not aware.
4. Awareness of fantasy experiences. Fantasy can be useful to discover more about ourselves. Fantasy can enable us to imagine, guess, play hunches, and try out things we are not experiencing now.

One unmistakable fact about awareness is that it is irreversible—you cannot become unaware once you are aware. You can attempt to repress or block awarenesses but they are difficult to block and it requires much energy to do so.

In the classroom, you can assist children in the process of intrapersonal communication by developing their awareness of themselves in the areas mentioned above. This process can teach children to trust in their awareness as an important tool for learning about themselves and the world around them.

Another important principle of intrapersonal communications is that of "here and now." This is a way of establishing a continuum of awareness and adding a new dimension of time and space to that continuum. Starting with what I am aware of in the present, I can then move to the future through use of fantasy awareness and move to the past from the perspective of how the past is affecting me in the present.

INTERNAL AWARENESS

Ways We Talk to Ourselves

One of the most common ways people trap themselves is by the words they use when they talk to themselves. We say "I have to," "I can't," "I should," and act as if someone else were telling us what to do and what not to do. Most people talk to themselves in very critical ways and don't know how to give themselves very many positive messages. Listen to and observe your thoughts about yourself for about ten minutes and check how many thoughts are critical and how many are nurturing.

All phrases like "have to," "should," and "ought to" imply that you have no choice. Make a list of things that you do that you think of as "have to's. "Start each one with "I have to . . ."; then, after you have completed the list, change the beginning of each one to "I choose to. . .'' This can be very useful in helping you to take responsibility for the choices you make instead of acting as if you were forced to make them.

Listening to the ways that students talk to you about themselves gives you some clues as to how they talk to themselves. Confront inappropriate critical words by saying: "You meant to say you choose to do that, didn't you?"

Ways to Stay in Touch with Feelings

Feelings are the basic level of awareness and are necessary for effective thinking and problem solving. They provide the energy required for people to know what they need and want.

Most people are not in touch with the feelings that underlie their thoughts. According to Hendricks (1975), any unobserved feeling symbolizes into a thought that actually distorts the feeling. We then act from a thought that is not accurately reflective of the underlying feeling. If people can be taught to see their feelings as they are, they will be more centered in their actions.

One way to help students in this process is to take time during the school day and have them stop what they are doing and tune into their feelings. Ask them "What are your feelings right now? How do you experience them?" Example: "I am feeling angry because I can't figure out this problem and I am experiencing the anger as tightness in my jaws."

Once students have learned to identify their feelings and know how the feelings are experienced, they can then be taught to integrate feelings and thoughts. One way to do this is to give a person permission to fully experience the feeling in his/her body, then to let it go, and then to himself or herself give positive messages for having the feeling and letting it go (Golas, 1974). This allows a person not only to experience the feeling fully but also to accept or "own" that feeling in its purest form.

Ways to Listen to the Body

The body is sending out signals constantly, but most people don't know how to listen to these signals and make use of them. Much is yet to be discovered about how we can bring all bodily functions under conscious control through increased awareness and biofeedback devices. We do know, however, that the structure of the body is very malleable and can be changed through the function of increased awareness.

One important fact about the notion of control of bodily functions and sensations is that it teaches people that they are responsible for what they are experiencing. For example, if you are experiencing tension in your back it is not correct to say "My back is hurting me." Rather, you should say "I am tensing my back and hurting myself."

Muscle tension in our bodies is usually chronic and because of that often goes unnoticed. Ask students to close their eyes while lying down and pay attention to any tension they are experiencing. Then get them to exaggerate the tension so they can feel it more acutely. After this level of awareness has been reached, ask them to own the experience ("I'm tensing my arm and hurting myself"), then release the tension and focus their awareness on completely relaxing that muscle and again owning the experience ("I'm relaxing my arm and making myself feel good").

EXTERNAL AWARENESS

Most people need to be taught to listen to their surroundings and to restore contact with those things going on outside of them. One way to help students do this is to ask them to focus their awareness on objects in their environment and let each object speak to them. Example: "I am the chalkboard and you write on me sometimes but someone usually erases it."

PAST AWARENESS

Feelings associated with past experiences that haven't been integrated tend to crowd into our present awareness often at crucial times. These unintegrated feelings from our past are still pushing into our awareness in order to give us the opportunity to integrate them.

Most unintegrated feelings from our past call up images of situations involving parents, teachers, or other adults. One way to assist students in this process of integration is to ask them to imagine a dialogue with one of their parents. Say to them: "With your eyes closed, picture one of your parents sitting in front of you. Notice as many things as you can about him (clothing, facial expression). How do you feel as you look at your parent? Tell him all the things that you never told him. Express everything that is on your mind that you have held back from saying, being aware of your feelings and your body." (Take five minutes to do this.)

"Then become your parent and respond: 'How do you feel toward your child? Tell your child how you feel.'" (Five minutes).

"Switch places and become yourself again, this time telling your parent what you need and want from him. Be specific about what it is you are wanting. Reverse roles and respond to what your child has said. Then tell your child what you want from him.

"Now switch again and tell your parent what you appreciate in him. Be specific. Then become your parent and respond. Now tell your child what you appreciate in him. Continue this dialogue as long as you want, dealing with issues and feelings you are hanging on to from the past."

If your students do this, eventually they will let go of the unintegrated feelings, give up making demands that their parents be different, and forgive them for their faults. This is an extremely important process for everyone to go through in order to restore his own power and let go of the past.

FANTASY AWARENESS

Fantasy can be a way that people avoid contact with the here and now. Most of us can spend a lot of our time worrying or hoping and planning for events and things that will never happen. Fantasy can be a valuable tool in the classroom, though, as long as it is integrated into the here and now and supports or extends our present awarenesses. If fantasy is split off from the present, it becomes merely an escape from the unpleasant experiences of daily living.

Full awareness involves identification with what you are experiencing in the here and now, whether you like the experience or not. When you have achieved that level of awareness with yourself and with others, then you can utilize fantasy to extend the here and now and integrate more into your experience of the present.

Unintegrated emotions and fantasies around them interfere with being in the here and now and being open to present experiences. Children need to learn how to develop, expand, and utilize fantasy awareness in learning about themselves and the world.

One important skill that children need is to learn how to distinguish between reality and fantasy in ways that don't discourage fantasy. A child who makes up a "pretend story" needs to hear that it's ok to do that. He or she should be encouraged to look at the real parts and the fantasy parts without making fantasy bad.

One activity that a teacher can utilize almost at any time in teaching content is to ask "What would happen if . . ." questions. For instance, "What would happen if you had eyes on the back of your head instead of on the front of your head?" or "What if the letter *e* were outlawed and when you wrote something you had to leave it out?")

In doing this kind of activity with a group it is important that everyone be given a chance to express to another person what he or she fantasized. In large groups have students pair off and share their fantasies. It is also important to model ways to be open and accepting in sharing fantasies.

If children have permission to fantasize and share fantasies, you as the teacher will be in a position to help them deal with scary fantasies and unintegrated feelings. Through use of regular small-group sharing sessions you can work with fantasies and feelings that need to be integrated. One example involved a four-year-old boy whose mother worked for the Forest Service. His father had been killed in a plane crash when he was a baby. The teacher noticed that at times he would fight and be mean to other children. He reported in a sharing session that every time his mother went into the forest overnight, as she did at times as part of her work, he would get very frightened that something would happen to her and she wouldn't come back. The teacher listened to the feelings and said, "You are afraid she won't come back and you will be left all alone." Then she held the child in her lap, comforted him, and asked what he thought he could do to feel less afraid. He came up with several ideas like "Tell Mommy not to go," but finally decided to tell her he was scared and ask her to take good care of herself so she would come back. The teacher talked to the parent several days later and found out that the child had dealt with his scary feelings with her and that they had had a beautiful experience sharing their feelings. After this there was a sharp reduction in the boy's fighting behavior at school, and the teacher checked on his feelings each time his mother went away for a day or two.

INTRAPERSONAL PROBLEM-SOLVING STRAGEGIES

At time we have problems that we have to work out ourselves and not in a problem-solving session with another person. We face decisions, choices, and problems where we have to communicate with ourselves.

There are a number of strategies that are useful in this process. Consider the following structure:

The problem or decision is _____
_____

My choices seem to be _____
_____

I believe it is wrong to _____
        right to _____
My mother or father would say _____
              and do _____
           and feel _____
The facts that I already have are _____
_____

The facts that I need to get are _____

My basic feelings about this are _____
_____

The feelings I'm supposed to have about this are _____
_____

My hunch is _____

My fantasy about solving this problem is _____
_____

TRANSPERSONAL COMMUNICATION

Teachers who have developed a classroom climate where effective interpersonal and intrapersonal communication is present have established the atmosphere necessary for transpersonal communication to occur. Transpersonal communication is designed to expand all human abilities and is best represented as the whole that is greater than the sum of its parts. It includes all effective interpersonal and intrapersonal communication as means to reaching higher levels of awareness and functioning. Effective interpersonal communication and intrapersonal communication are necessary to help people make contact with and break through cultural roles, ego defenses, body defenses, and unintegrated feelings. Through these processes a person can establish and maintain contact with his inner core, where unity with all life energy occurs. Figure 3 illustrates these processes and the conditions necessary for transpersonal communication to occur.

**Figure 3.
The Transpersonal
Person**

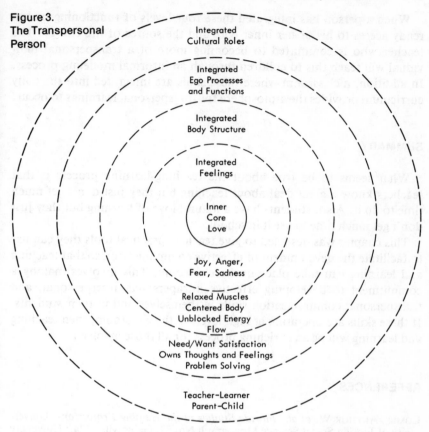

The transpersonal individual has integrated cultural roles to the extent that he or she can be both teacher and learner or both parent and child. The roles are flexible and adaptable to the situation. At the second level, the ego functions are free from the usual defenses and operate to enable the person to get needs and wants satisfied without discounting. The person who is free from ego defenses can readily "own" his or her thoughts and feelings and engage in effective problem solving.

At the third level, the body reflects the integration. Muscles are relaxed, the body maintains a centered position, and there is an unblocked energy flow throughout. At the emotional level, the person is in touch with basic feelings and is able to utilize these feelings in thinking and solving problems.

When a person has integrated these four levels of functioning he has ready access to his or her inner core and the source of life energy. The teacher who is committed to becoming more of a transpersonal individual will teach this to children through an informal modeling process. In addition, a classroom where these skills are integrated into the daily curriculum provides the atmosphere for transpersonal learnings to occur.

SUMMARY

What seems to be true about the teaching-learning process is that teachers know a great deal about teaching but they just don't get much time to do it. Also, students have a natural love of learning but they just don't get much time to use it in school.

This chapter was designed to give teachers practical tools they can use to facilitate the development of effective communication so that teaching and learning can take place in the classroom. This involves making a commitment to developing effective intrapersonal, interpersonal, and transpersonal communication skills in themselves and in their students. If these skills are operating at high levels in the classroom, then teaching and learning will be an enriching process for all those involved.

REFERENCES

COMBS, ARTHUR W. *et al., Florida Studies in the Helping Professions.* University of Florida Social Science Monograph No. 37. Gainesville, Fla.: University of Florida Press, 1969.

FALZETT, WILLIAM, and JEAN MAXWELL, *OK Childing and Parenting.* El Paso, Tex.: Transactional Analysis Insitute of El Paso, 1974.

GOLAS, THADDEUS, *The Lazy Man's Guide to Enlightenment.* Palo Alto: The Seed Center, 1972.

GORDON, THOMAS, *Teacher Effectiveness Training.* New York: Peter H. Wyden, 1974.

HENDRICKS, C. G., *Integral Therapy.* Unpublished manuscript, 1975.

HOLT, JOHN, *Escape From Childhood.* New York: Ballantine Books, 1974.

LEVIN, PAM, "A Think Structure for Feeling Fine Faster," *Transactional Analysis Journal,* January, 1973.

LOWEN, ALEXANDER, *Bioenergetics.* New York: Coward, McCann and Geoghegan, 1975.

MASLOW, ABRAHAM, *The Further Reaches of Human Nature.* New York: Viking, 1971.

MAY, ROLLO, *Power and Innocence. New York: W.W. Norton, 1972.*

SCHIFF, AARON W., and JACQUI SCHIFF, "Passivity," *Transpersonal Analysis Journal,* January, 1971.

EDUCATION AS A TRANSPERSONAL EXPERIENCE

You cannot teach transpersonal experience. You can hear about it, you can see it happening, and you can experience it. You can also get a feeling for it so that your own relationships allow it to occur more easily and more often. As a teacher, you can create an environment which facilitates it.

Throughout this book we have drawn from situations which are close to the normal school setting. Here we go farther afield. Out intention is to give you a clearer vision of the broad range of educational possibilities that open up transpersonal vistas.

These final selections are an opportunity for you to enjoy a variety of examples and points of view. All the selections are reflections or illustrations of how persons concerned with transpersonal teaching go about their business.

For learning to take root there must be the proper situation, the proper teacher, the proper tools, and the proper students. The selections here offer glimpses of moments in which all of the criteria have been met.

Please do not "learn" from reading what follows. Simply enjoy and perhaps reflect on what you read. We would appreciate it if you would *share with us any other passages you have read or experiences you have had that have been meaningful in your own education.*

Gurdjieff as
Elementary Teacher

Fritz Peters

Georges Gurdjieff, a Russian philosopher who had a wide-ranging influence in Europe and the United States during the twenties and thirties, taught that people were "asleep," unaware of much of their daily life, routinized into creatures of habit.

Students all over the world continue to practice the principles set down by this man described as a superb and extremely difficult teacher. Fritz Peters was sent to Gurdjieff's institute by his avant-garde guardians. Here he recalls his first meeting with this most unorthodox "elementary" teacher.

I met and talked to Georges Gurdjieff for the first time in 1924, on a Saturday afternoon in June, at the Château du Prieuré in Fontainebleau-Avon, France. Although the reasons for my being there were not very clear in my mind—I was eleven at the time—my memory of that meeting is still brilliantly clear.

It was a bright, sunny day. Gurdjieff was sitting by a small marble-topped table, shaded by a striped umbrella, with his back to the château

"Gurdjieff as Elementary Teacher" (editors' title). From Fritz Peters, *Boyhood with Gurdjieff* (New York: E. P. Dutton and Co., Inc., 1964), pp. 5-8; 162-64. Reprinted by permission of the author.

proper, facing a large expanse of formal lawns and flower beds. I had to sit on the terrace of the château, behind him, for some time before I was summoned to his side for an interview. I had, actually, seen him once before, in New York the previous winter, but I did not feel that I had "met" him. My only memory of that prior time was that I had been frightened of him; partly because of the way he looked at—or through—me, and partly because of his reputation. I had been told that he was at least a "prophet"—at most, something very close to the "second coming of Christ."

Meeting any version of a "Christ" is an event, and this meeting was not one to which I looked forward. Facing the presence not only did not appeal to me—I dreaded it.

The actual meeting did not measure up to my fears. "Messiah" or not, he seemed to me a simple, straightforward man. He was not surrounded by any halo, and while his English was heavily accented, he spoke far more simply than the Bible had led me to expect. He made a vague gesture in my direction, told me to sit down, called for coffee, and then asked me why I was there. I was relieved to find that he seemed to be an ordinary human being, but I was troubled by the question. I felt sure that I was supposed to give him an *important* answer; that I should have some excellent reason. Having none, I told him the truth: That I was there because I had been brought there.

He then asked me why I wanted to be there, to study at his school. Once more I was only able to answer that it was all beyond my control—I had not been consulted, I had been, as it were, transported to that place. I remember my strong impulse to lie to him, and my equally strong feeling that I could not lie to him. I felt sure that he knew the truth in advance. The only question that I answered less than honestly was when he asked me if I wanted to stay there and to study with him. I said that I did, which was not essentially true. I said it because I knew that it was expected of me. It seems to me, now, that any child would have answered as I did. Whatever the Prieuré might represent to adults (and the literal name of the school was "The Gurdjieff Institute for the Harmonious Development of Man"), I felt that I was experiencing the equivalent of being interviewed by the principal of a high school. Children went to school, and I subscribed to the general agreement that no child would tell his teacher-to-be that he did not want to go to school. The only thing that surprised me was that I was asked the question.

Gurdjieff then asked me two more questions:

1. What do you think life is?
and
2. What do you want to know?

I answered the first question by saying: "I think life is something that is handed to you on a silver platter, and it is up to you (me) to do something with it." This answer touched off a long discussion about the phrase "on a silver platter," including a reference by Gurdjieff to the head of John the Baptist. I retreated—it felt like a retreat—and modified the phrase to the effect that life was a "gift," and this seemed to please him.

The second question (What do you want to know?) was simpler to answer. My words were: "I want to know everything."

Gurdjieff replied immediately: "You cannot know everything. Everything about what?"

I said: "Everything about man," and then added: "In English I think it is called psychology or maybe philosophy."

He sighed then, and after a short silence said: "You can stay. But your answer makes life difficult for me. I am the only one who teaches what you ask. You make more work for me."

Since my childish aims were to conform and to please, I was disconcerted by his answer. The last thing I wanted to do was to make life more difficult for anyone—it seemed to me that it was difficult enough already. I said nothing in reply to this, and he went on to tell me that in addition to learning "everything" I would also have the opportunity to study lesser subjects, such as languages, mathematics, various sciences, and so forth. He also said that I would find that his was not the usual school: "Can learn many things here that other schools not teach." He then patted my shoulder benevolently.

I use the word "benevolently" because the gesture was of great importance to me at the time. I longed for approval from some higher authority. To receive such "approval" from this man who was considered by other adults to be a "prophet," "seer," and/or a "Messiah" —and approval in such a simple, friendly gesture—was unexpected and heartwarming. I beamed.

His manner changed abruptly. He struck the table with one fist, looked at me with great intensity, and said: "Can you promise to do something for me?"

His voice and the look he had given me were frightening and also exciting. I felt both cornered and challenged. I answered him with one word, a firm "Yes."

He gestured towards the expanse of lawns before us: "You see this grass?"

"Yes."

"I give you work. You must cut this grass, with machine, every week."

I looked at the lawns, the grass spreading before us into what appeared to me infinity. It was, without any doubt, a prospect of more work in one week than I had ever contemplated in my life. Again, I said "Yes."

He struck the table with his fist for a second time. "You must promise on your God." His voice was deadly serious. "You must promise that you will do this thing no matter what happens."

I looked at him, questioning, respectful, and with considerable awe. No lawn—not even these (there were four of them)—had ever seemed important to me before. "I promise," I said earnestly.

"Not just promise," he reiterated. "Must promise you will do no matter what happens, no matter who try stop you. Many things can happen in life."

For a moment his words conjured up visions of terrifying arguments over the mowing of these lawns. I foresaw great emotional dramas taking place in the future on account of these lawns and of myself. Once again, I promised. I was as serious as he was then. I would have died, if necessary, in the act of mowing the lawns.

My feeling of dedication was obvious, and he seemed satisfied. He told me to begin work on Monday, and then dismissed me. I don't think I realized it at the time—that is, the sensation was new to me—but I left him with the feeling that I had fallen in love; whether with the man, the lawns, or myself, did not matter. My chest was expanded far beyond its normal capacity. I, a child, an unimportant cog in the world which belonged to adults, had been asked to perform something that was apparently vital.

[Later in his education, Fritz was given the job of tending the herb garden.]

What with adolescence, lack of supervision, lack of interest, and just plain laziness, I managed to do as little work as possible in the Herb

Garden. I avoided going there except when it was necessary for me to bring various herbs to the kitchen. When the quality of the herbs became noticeably poorer and when I was at times unable even to supply a small quantity of some particular herb, someone must have taken it upon themselves to investigate the garden and report their findings to Gurdjieff.

The result was that Gurdjieff made a personal inspection of the garden with me, walking up and down between all the small beds, examining every plant. When he had finished he told me that as far as he could see, I had done absolutely nothing at all there in the way of work. I had to admit that I had done very little work, but defended myself to the extent of pointing out that I had done some occasional weeding. He shook his head and said that in view of the state of the garden it would be better not to defend myself at all. He then assigned several of the children to work with me in the garden until it was in proper shape, and instructed me as to what had to be done to the various plants: hoeing between the rows, trimming certain plants, dividing and replanting others.

Although the children were very annoyed with me for having shirked my own work and thereby caused them to have to work on "my" garden, they all pitched in and we carried out Gurdjieff's orders very easily and quickly. It was a very small plot of land and it could not have taken us more than a day or two. When we had finished the work, Gurdjieff pronounced it satisfactory, complimented all the other children on their work, and said that he wanted to have a talk with me, alone.

He first told me that I could see for myself that I had not performed a task that had been assigned to me, and that it had been necessary for him to intervene in my work and take measures to repair the damage that had been caused by my neglect. He said that this was a very good example of the way in which one person's failure to accomplish his duty could affect the general welfare of everyone else and that, while I might not think of herbs as important, they were important to him and were needed in the kitchen; also that I had caused him an unnecessary, if minor, expense because various plants had had to be purchased, which would not have been necessary if I had done my job properly.

He went on to say that it was true, in one sense, that the herb garden was not important; what was important, however, was to be responsible and to do one's work, particularly when that work could affect the welfare of others. However, there was another, still more important reason for accomplishing any assigned task, which was for one's own sake.

He spoke again about the exercise of "self-observation" and said that since man was a three-centred or three-brained being, it was necessary to do exercises and perform tasks that were valuable for all three centres, not just the physical or "motor" centre; that "self-observation" as I knew it was a purely physical exercise in that it consisted in the observation of one's physical body and its movements, gestures and manifestations.

He said that there were various important exercises having to do with "self-remembering" which was a very important aspect of his work. One of them was to conscientiously and with all one's concentration, try to remember, as on a movie film, everything that one had done during each entire day. This was to be done every night before going to sleep. The most important thing in the exercise was not to let the attention wander —by association. If one's attention did wander from the focus upon the image of oneself, then it was absolutely necessary to begin all over again at the beginning each time this happened—and it would, he warned, happen.

He talked to me for a very long time that morning, and emphasized the fact that everyone had, usually, a particular, recurring problem in life. He said that these particular problems were usually a form of laziness, and that I was to think about my laziness, which took a fairly obvious physical form, as in the case of the garden: I had simply put off doing anything in the garden until someone had taken notice of that fact. He said that he wanted me to think seriously about my laziness—not the outward form, which was not important, but to find out what it was. When you see that you are lazy, necessary find out what this laziness *is*. Because in some ways you already lazy for many years, can take even many years for you to find out what it is. Must ask yourself, whenever you see your own laziness: "What is this laziness in me?" If you ask this question seriously, and with concentration, is possible someday you will find answer. This important and very difficult work I give you now."

I thanked him for what he had said and added that I was sorry that I had not done my work in the garden and that I would do it properly in the future.

He brushed aside my thanks and said that it was useless to be sorry. "Is too late for that now, and is also too late to do good work in garden. In life never have second chance, only have one chance. You had one time to do good work in garden, for self; you not do, so now even if you work all your life, in this garden, cannot be same thing for you. But also important not be 'sorry' about this; can waste all life feeling sorry. There is valuable thing sometimes, thing you call remorse. If man have real remorse for something he do that is not good, this can be valuable; but if only sorry and say will do same thing better in future is waste of time. This time is already gone forever, this part of your life is finished, you cannot live over again. Not important if you do good work in garden now, because will do for wrong reasons—to try to repair damage which cannot be repaired ever. This serious thing. But also very serious not to waste time feeling sorry or feeling regret, this only waste even more time. Must learn in life, not to make such mistakes, and must understand that once made mistake is made forever.''

An Interview with One of Gurdjieff's Teachers

Rafael Lefort

In this selection a writer tracks down one of the people responsible for Gurdjieff's own transpersonal education, Hassan Effendi, who has some surprising things to say about the "curriculum" he taught.

". . . I taught Gurdjieff to breathe. I say this and you burst into a flood of how's, why's and ifs and buts and can I teach you? The answer is, I can but I will not."

"May I ask, Sheikh, why only breathing?"

"Only! Only! Stupid question! More stupid than to have asked why or how. Do you think that to learn to breathe correctly is easy? Does your shallow panting do more than supply your blood with the minimum amount of oxygen needed to keep that portion of your brain that you use alive? One of the functions of correct breathing is to carry the baraka to the farthest recess of the deep consciousness. Undeveloped men try to use thought or random action to affect the consciousness. Neither of these

"An Interview With One of Gurdjieff's Teachers" (editor's title). From Rafael Lefort, *The Teachers of Gurdjieff* (London: Gollancz, Ltd., 1970), pp. 62–65. Reprinted by permission of the publisher.

works as the dose and the direction and the intensity are not known to them. Only to breathe! Do you know how long it takes before you can be trained to take your first *real* breath? Months, even years, and then only when you *know* what you are aiming for.

"Gurdjieff came to me with a capacity to breathe and I taught him how to do it and how to breathe with his system, his consciousness and his entire being. You breathe to sustain your level of existence. Higher man breathes to maintain the breakthrough that he has made into a superior realm of being. Your ignorance, while not surprising, terrifies me. Gurdjieff stayed with me for twenty years. Yes, twenty years! Five months in Erzurum and the remainder of the time in rapport with me wherever he was learning to use his breath. Do you know what can be carried into your consciousness by your breath? Do you know why a Sheikh will breathe on a disciple? Do you know why a Sheikh breathes into the ear of a newly born child? Of course you do not! You put it down to magic, primitive symbols representing life, but the practical reasons, the deadly serious business of nourishing the inner conscious-ness, passes you by. Flows over your head, bent as it is over physiology, psychology, causative phenomena, theoretic ecstasies. You blind your-self, life does not blind you. You call out in your pitiful arrogance for enlightenment, you claim your right to it as a birthright. You earn it, my friend, you earn it by dedication, toil and discipline. A hundred years must a body travel until it is seasoned. A seeker does not become a real Sufi until the very marrow of his bones has been seasoned in the oven of reality! Talk less of 'only breathing' and see how pitifully unprepared you yourself are even to approach the concept of Existence! Your capacity to profit from anything is directly proportionate to the efficiency of your system.

"This is true physiologically as well as esoterically. You cannot, and you know it, expect your body to extract and process sugar if you have no pancreas, and yet, in your arrogant, intellectual way, you expect to be able to profit from the knowledge that others have bought for you. You want to use what you call the 'process of thought or logic' to pick over the whole and eat the parts that you consider nourishing. At best your thought processes are surface reactions, at worst you cannot absorb a reaction or thought before it is fallen upon, diluted, dissected and malformed by the infernal process that you call academic reasoning. Reason, you call it! Do you call it reasonable to gulp down great pieces of wisdom and regurgitate them in the form of theory, the speech and the drivelings of a raw mind? The so-called Age of Reason in Europe produced less reason, less *real* intellectual progress, than one day's activity by a developed man.

"You aspire, you dream, but you do not do! Tenacity is replaced by hair-splitting, courage by bluster, and disciplined thought by narrow, pedantic attempts at reason. Bend what little you have left of your intellect to practical activity, realising your severe shortcomings. Cease your diabolic 'examination of self.' Who am I? How many I's do I have? You have not the capacity at all to understand the concept of true self-examination. Follow a valid philosophy or condemn yourself to join the generations who have drowned themselves in the stagnant pools of slime that they call the reservoirs of reason and intellect!

"You have no reason, no intellect, do you understand? Even less have you of the catalytic substance that would allow you to use the reason and intellect that might just have survived the conditioning you have so warmly welcomed.

"Yes, I only taught Gurdjieff to breathe! No more, no less." . . .

The Hows and Whys of Power Points

Reshad Feild

Enlightenment can strike at the strangest times. Here, a ten-year-old boy learns an unforgettable lesson from a true transpersonal teacher.

. . . I was 10 years old and my family had an estate in the southern part of England. There was a gamekeeper on the estate who taught me all about the world of nature.

I would have to walk out with him with an unloaded gun on his rounds. and, once a week, when all the adults would assemble to slaughter whatever moved or flew, I would walk out with them, standing in line as they did, always my gun unloaded so that I could learn the discipline necessary to be a safe shot when I grew up.

Once a week the gamekeeper would take me out into the woods and teach me how to catch rabbits with my hands. To be able to do this it was essential that I could come to "think" like a rabbit, to know what instinct

Excerpted from "The Hows and Whys of Power Points," by Reshad Feild, in *East-West Journal,* IV, no. 5, June 1974, 26, 27, 35. Reprinted by permission of the *East-West Journal,* 31 Farnsworth St., Boston, Mass.

made it sit in this place or that place when it was not in its hole, how the weather affected it, and the time of the day.

Pretty soon I came to almost be able to put myself into the brain of that tiny creature.

The day came when I had to experiment with the actual catching of one of the rabbits that I had watched and loved for so long. "What you have to do," the gamekeeper said, "is to be able to know which way it is going to move before it does. . . . You have to be quicker than the rabbit, and if you are very, very aware you will be where it will be before it has moved. . . ."

I stamped my foot in the same way that the rabbit does in time of danger, and then threw myself in the direction that I knew he would move. In a time quicker than I would have thought possible, the rabbit was struggling in my arms.

"Now you must kill it as you have been taught," the keeper said to me.

How could I ever forget that moment? Through loving the animal kingdom I had come to learn about it and to understand it, and now I was confronted with a similar experience to that of Castaneda's with Don Juan, the conscious transmutation of energy. As the rabbit died it was as though I was transported into another world. Everything shone, the trees gave off a silver light, there was a sense of recognition in every leaf, every plant, and in the earth itself. I knew then that I was not inside my body, but my body was *inside me.* I was participating in the great drama of life, and for a 10-year-old boy, shot into the realization of the Oneness of all life, the experience left a mark that has never been forgotten.

The Education of
the Buddhist Child

The Reverend Jiyu Kennett, Roshi

*The Reverend Kennett, who has spent much time in Japan, describes education
and childrearing among contemporary Buddhists.*

With young Buddhists growing up around us by the score and more and
more of the members of the Society marrying and having their own
children, not to mention interest in the education of the young on the
part of the Sufis and other friendly religious organizations, I have been
asked to discuss, or rather delineate, the usual method of education of
the Buddhist child throughout the east. There are certain differences with
regard to the approach to the education of Buddhists as opposed to
members of other religions and I think these are basic to a Buddhist
education anywhere, whether it is in the east or west. So, first and fore-
most, I would like to point out what is probably obvious to most of you,
but which is certainly not obvious to the average parent in England, for
example, where I myself was brought up; and that is that the child must

"The Education of the Buddhist Child" by The Reverend Jiyu Kennett, Roshi. From the
Journal of the Zen Mission Society, 5, no. 12 (December 1974), 12–16. Reprinted by
permission of the publisher.

be cherished—not merely looked after or even loved but cherished. However foolish its comments, however childish, however silly, however babyish, the child is trying to express itself and must never be thought of as something that is *needing* to be educated rather as that which has within itself all the knowledge that matters that ever was. And it is our duty as educators to unlock the doors of that knowledge so that the child may *experience* and *express* what it already knows.

Buddhism, unlike some other religions, does not believe in original sin. Therefore it places no guilt on the child from the moment it is conceived. Instead, it says that we are simply born and later, as a result of what we do with ourselves, of what happens to us and as a result of our going into dual thinking—right and wrong—"this is right, that is wrong; this is good, this is bad"—we educate ourselves out of our original oneness of mind into a duality which, at a later date, we have to transcend if we are to be able to do anything whatsoever to overcome the spiritual illnesses our education has generated.

The average child going to school in the west is taught from the moment it enters, "Now, you are a child and I am *the* teacher. *You* do *not* know and *I do* know." I can certainly remember, and I am sure most of my readers can remember also, the moment when something inside us was almost killed or, at least, shut off by a watertight door. We were perfectly all right until the moment when it was made quite clear to us that we did not know and that the teacher *did*. For this was the moment when doubt entered our minds—and fear entered them because we had been told that we were inadequate—and we were already in the toils of duality.

Buddhist education does not do this. The Buddhist teacher, if he is a real teacher, says. "This child knows all, as indeed I know all, but he cannot yet express it and I can only express it partially. Therefore he and I are on the same road. I have been going along it for a little longer than he has and I will try to go at the speed he is going at so that he may catch up with me and, perhaps, be able to surpass me—who knows?" So it is the duty of the Buddhist teacher to get his egocentric self out of the way to a very, very great extent so that the education of the child may be a free and beautiful thing, untrammeled by "Look at what *I* have achieved in *my* educating of this child!" It is the child that does the educating of itself by using its experiences to fall back on later; the child that makes the running; and the child that matters—we are all children in the Buddha Nature. When we say, as teachers, "*I* know and *you* do not," we are really saying, "*Our* Buddha Nature is better than *your* Buddha

Nature"; thus is set up duality, self, fear and inadequacy. If, on the other hand, we say, "Your Buddha Nature and our Buddha Nature are one but there is a difference between us because you are smaller than us and we are older than you; therefore we have run a little farther but we will come back to help you run as far," the difference in our attitude of mind, the difference in the attitude of the child to learning, is phenomenal.

I am often asked, "How do you teach meditation to children and what is the best age to start at?" In the east the average child is taught to meditate as soon as it is possible for it to sit upright; i.e., around one or two years old. No doctrine is put into the child's head. The mother and father, and the rest of the family, will sit quietly in front of the family altar; the child, without being restrained, will either sit for a few moments or roll around on the floor with the parents taking no notice. The parents thus express their knowledge of the child's latent understanding and do not treat it as less than themselves. In a very short time the child wants to sit like the parents, as do, interestingly enough, the dog and cat. I have sat down to meditate and my cat has come up, looked at the wall and then sat down to look at it with me. Thus, if the parents meditate, the child will meditate too. I have seen children at the age of two and a half doing formal meditation in the laymen's meditation hall in Sojiji— and doing a wonderful job. I have photographs of them. These children do a meditation so pure and exquisite it is unbelievable to watch; but they would not be able to discuss the Buddha Nature with you, nor would they be able to put into words the doctrine of the Trikaya—nor would they be able to explain the "all is one" and the "all is different" that their little bodies express. Their explanations are not as the world understands explanations. And yet every part of their bodies will express the "all is one" and the "all is different"—they will express the Buddha Nature for they have learned to meditate with their whole being untrammeled by duality. They are indeed *whole* creatures and can teach us much.

The education of the child starts prior to birth, on the very night of its conception. The attitude of mind of the parents—whether they are in a selfish mood, simply wishing to gratify their own pleasure, or whether they are wishing to produce a child which both of them will love—will affect the child at a later date. The Buddha Nature, which is within all of us, knows what is happening to itself, and the future child is conditioned by the attitudes of mind of the parents at conception. Therefore, education does not even begin at the first look that passes between the mother and the child; it begins with the look in the eyes of the two parents, whether they be full of lust or whether they be full of self-less love. There used to be an old saying that there was such a thing as a "love child" in existence. It is unfortunate that it became a derogatory term, pertaining to a child born out of wedlock.

From what I have said, therefore, in a very real sense, "The sins of the fathers are visited upon the children," and the children are born carrying the karmic load which the parents have put upon them; their teachers later force them to continue to carry it. This is indeed a great grief. Parents should know well what it is they do on the night of conception and make no mistakes. They should also know well why it is that a child may ask, at a later date, with genuine grief in his heart, the old Zen kōan, "Why did you beget me? Why was I born? Before my parents conceived me, what was my original face?" These kōans can be taken on many levels and can be understood by many, many means. The next step is for the parent to cherish the child, not merely love it; the parent must always be open to the child, never sneering at, or belittling its efforts, never looking down upon it, from first seeing it at birth until it becomes an adult.

Those of you who have read my diary will remember certain incidents in my own childhood: for instance when I came running home to my family, longing to tell them what I had learned, and the supercilious laughter when I explained, as best I could, what my lessons had been. "Oh, how clever you are," I was told, and something snapped shut inside me. This would never happen in a Buddhist family or school that is properly run. However childish the remarks, however silly even, the child will always be treated as if it is a serious human being. As the child gets steadily older the strictness with which it is treated by the teachers increases gradually, but it is never a strictness that is, in any way, derogatory of the child's ability. Even the stupidest child is fully accepted as having the Buddha Nature; it is embraced within the Buddha Mind and never made to feel inferior. "There are some Buddhas that are tall, some short, some fat, some thin, some bright, some stupid," say the scriptures. Unless you can see the Buddha in the little child who comes to you with his "silly" story, as we *great* grown-ups consider it; unless you can see the Buddha in the little boy with his hand in the cookie jar and unless you can see the Buddha when you spank him—and spank him with love and cherish him in your heart whilst doing it—you will not be able to educate the Buddhist child.

Formal education starts the moment the child is first held in his mother's arms. The openness within her heart and within her eyes are the beginning of that formal education. That openness must remain; the full acceptance of the oneness of the mother and child must also be the full acceptance of the oneness of the teacher and pupil. My advice to those who educate anyone is, "Remember, there is no difference between you and the pupil other than that of age. Neither of you possess more than the other; there is only the illusion of knowledge. Unless you understand that mental knowledge is an illusion in the religious sense you will never be able to impart anything whatsoever of real value."

We need to remember that age barriers are created by pride—"I am older than you, therefore I know more than you"; to which the young reply with the words, "We are younger than you and we don't care whether you know more than we do or not because we are younger and have more time to learn." So, by being proud, the old are despised, and so is their knowledge; and, by despising the old, the young are deprived of the passed-down practical wisdom of the ages. If, from the very beginning, education is understood as starting with unselfish conception and then the loving and the cherishing, not only of the child when it is your own, but when it is your pupil, there is no danger whatsoever of there ever being an age barrier and education is seen to be a means of growing together within the Spirit of the Buddhas.

From *On Having No Head*

D. E. Harding

Education is usually concerned with teaching people how to think. Douglas Harding's article suggests that perhaps we should be helping them to stop thinking.

The best day of my life—my rebirthday, so to speak—was when I found I had no head. This is not a literary gambit, a witticism designed to arouse interest at any cost. I mean it in all seriousness: *I have no head.*

It was eighteen years ago, when I was thirty-three, that I made the discovery. Though it certainly came out of the blue, it did so in response to an urgent enquiry; I had for several months been absorbed in the question: what am I? The fact that I happened to be walking in the Himalayas at the time probably had little to do with it; though in that country unusual states of mind are said to come more easily. However that may be, a very still clear day, and a view from the ridge where I stood, over misty blue valleys to the highest mountain range in the world,

From *On Having No Head: A Contribution to Zen in the West,* by D. E. Harding (New York: Harper & Row, Publishers, Inc., 1963), 5-7. Reprinted by permission of The Buddhist Society of London, England.

with Kangchenjunga and Everest unprominent among its snow-peaks, made a setting worthy of the grandest vision.

What actually happened was something absurdly simple and unspectacular: I stopped thinking. A peculiar quiet, an odd kind of alert limpness or numbness, came over me. Reason and imagination and all mental chatter died down. For once, words really failed me. Past and future dropped away. I forgot who and what I was, my name, manhood, animalhood, all that could be called mine. It was as if I had been born that instant, brand new, mindless, innocent of all memories. There existed only the Now, that present moment and what was clearly given in it. To look was enough. And what I found was khaki trouserlegs terminating downwards in a pair of brown shoes, khaki sleeves terminating sideways in a pair of pink hands, and a khaki shirtfront terminating upwards in—absolutely nothing whatever! Certainly not in a head.

It took me no time at all to notice that this nothing, this hole where a head should have been, was no ordinary vacancy, no mere nothing. On the contrary, it was very much occupied. It was a vast emptiness vastly filled, a nothing that found room for everything—room for grass, trees, shadowy distant hills, and far above them snow-peaks like a row of angular clouds riding the blue sky. I had lost a head and gained a world.

It was all, quiet literally, breathtaking. I seemed to stop breathing altogether, absorbed in the Given. Here it was, this superb scene, brightly shining in the clear air, alone and unsupported, mysteriously suspended in the void, and (and *this* was the real miracle, the wonder and delight) utterly free of "me," unstained by any observer. Its total presence was my total absence, body and soul. Lighter than air, clearer than glass, altogether released from myself, I was nowhere around.

Yet in spite of the magical and uncanny quality of this vision, it was no dream, no esoteric revelation. Quite the reverse: it felt like a sudden waking from the sleep of ordinary life, an end to dreaming. It was self-luminous reality for once swept clean of all obscuring mind. It was the revelation, at long last, of the perfectly obvious. It was a lucid moment in a confused life-history. It was a ceasing to ignore something which (since early childhood at any rate) I had always been too busy or too clever to see. It was naked, uncritical attention to what had all along been staring me in the face—my utter facelessness. In short, it was all perfectly simple and plain and straightforward, beyond argument, thought, and words. There arose no questions, no reference beyond the experience itself, but only peace and a quiet joy, and the sensation of having dropped an intolerable burden.

The Joy of Fishes

Chuang Tzu

Thomas Merton, who freely translated this selection, has written: "Chuang Tzu is not concerned with words and formulas about reality, but with the direct existential grasp of reality in itself." The original was written in China about the third or fourth century B.C. As another Taoist teacher put it, "Nothing is gained by speculation. Things are always as they are."

Merton, a Trappist contemplative, was deeply interested in the relationship between Eastern and Western mysticism.

> Chuang Tzu and Hui Tzu
> Were crossing Hao river
> By the dam.
>
> Chuang said:
> "See how free
> The fishes leap and dart:
> That is their happiness."

Hui replied:
"Since you are not a fish
How do you know
What makes fishes happy?"

Chuang said:
"Since you are not I
How can you possibly know
That I do not know
What makes fishes happy?"

Hui argued:
"If I, not being you,
Cannot know what you know
It follows that you
Not being a fish
Cannot know what they know."

Chuang said:
"Wait a minute!
Let us get back
To the original question.
What you asked me was
'How do you know
What makes fishes happy?'
From the terms of your question
You evidently know I know
What makes fishes happy.

"I know the joy of fishes
In the river
Through my own joy, as I go walking
Along the same river."

How Knowledge Was Earned

Idries Shah

The teaching story, used widely as an educational tool in the East, has only recently come to be widely appreciated in the West. Stories such as these are said to speak to students on deeper than ordinary levels.

Once upon a time there was a man who decided that he needed knowledge. He set off to look for it, bending his steps towards the house of a learned man.

When he got there he said: "Sufi, you are a wise man! Let me have a portion of your knowledge, so that I may grow it and become worthwhile, for I feel that I am nothing."

The Sufi said: "I can give you knowledge in exchange for something which I myself need. Go and bring me a small carpet, for I have to give it to someone who will then be able to further our holy work."

So the man went off, looking for someone who could let him have thread. When he arrived at the hut of a spinner-woman, he said to her:

"Spinner-woman, give me thread. I have to have it for the carpet-man, who will give me a carpet which I will give to a Sufi, who will give it to a man who has to do our holy work. In exchange I will get knowledge, which I want."

The woman immediately answered: "You need thread, what about me? Away with this talk about you, and your Sufi and your carpet-man and the man who has to have the carpet. What about me? I need goat-hair to make thread. Get me some and you can have your thread."

So the man went off, until he came to a goat-herd, and he told him his needs. The goat-herd said: "What about me? You need goat-hair to buy knowledge, I need goats to provide the hair. Get me a goat and I shall help you."

So the man went off, looking for someone who sold goats. When he found such a man he told him his difficulties, and the man said: "What do I know about knowledge, or thread or carpets? All I know is that everyone seems to be looking after his own interests. Let us instead talk about my needs, and if you can satisfy them, then we will talk about goats, and you can think about knowledge all you wish."

"What are your needs?" asked the man.

"I need a pen to keep my goats in at night, because they are straying all over the place. Get me one and then talk about your having a goat or two."

So the man went off to look for a pen. His inquiries led him to a carpenter, who said: "Yes, I can make a pen for the man who needs one. As for the rest, you could have spared me the details, for I am just not interested in carpets or knowledge and the like. But I have a desire, and it is in your interests to help me gain it, otherwise I need not help you with your pen."

"And what is that desire?" asked the man.

"I want to get married and nobody will marry me, it seems. See whether you can arrange a wife for me, and then we will talk about your problems."

So the man went off, and after making exhaustive inquiries he found a woman who said: "I know a young woman who has no other desire than to marry just such a carpenter as you describe. In fact she has been thinking about him all her life. It must be some sort of miracle that he does exist and that she can hear of him through you and me. But what about me? Everyone wants what he wants, and people seem to need things, or want things, or imagine that they need help, or really want help, but nobody has yet said anything about *my* needs."

"And what are your needs?" asked the man.

"I want only one thing," said the woman," and I have wanted it all my life. Help me to get it, and you can have anything I have. The thing that I want, as I have experienced everything else, is—knowledge."

"But we cannot have knowledge without a carpet," said the man.

"I do not know what knowledge is, but I am sure that it is not a carpet," said the woman.

"No," said the man, seeing that he had to be patient, "but with the girl for the carpenter we can get the pen for the goats. With the pen for the goats we can get the goat-hair for the spinner. With the goat-hair we can get the thread. With the thread we can get the carpet. With the carpet we can get the knowledge."

"It sounds preposterous to me," said the woman, "and I for one am not going to go to those lengths."

In spite of his entreaties, she sent him away.

These difficulties and the confusion which they caused him first made him almost despair of the human race. He wondered whether he could use knowledge when he got it, and he wondered why all those people were only thinking of their own interests. And slowly he began to think only of the carpet.

One day this man was wandering through the streets of a market-town, muttering to himself.

A certain merchant heard him, and drew near to catch his words. The man was saying: "A carpet is needed to give to a man so that he may be able to do this holy work of ours."

The merchant realized that there was something exceptional about the wanderer, and addressed him:

"Wandering dervish, I do not understand your chant, but I have deep respect for one such as you, who has embarked upon the Path of Truth. Please help me, if you will, for I know that the people of the Sufi way have a special function in society."

The wanderer looked up and saw the distress on the merchant's face and said to him: "I am suffering and I have suffered. You are undoubtedly in trouble, but I have nothing. I cannot even get a piece of thread when I want it. But ask me and I will do anything that I can."

"Know, fortunate man!" said the merchant, "that I have an only and beautiful daughter. She is suffering from an illness which has caused her to languish. Come to her and perhaps you will be able to effect a cure."

Such was the man's distress and so high were his hopes that the wanderer followed him to the girl's bedside.

As soon as she saw him, she said: "I do not know who you are, but I feel you may be able to help me. In any case there is nobody else. I am in love with such-and-such a carpenter." And she named the man whom the traveller had asked to make the pen for the goats.

"Your daughter wants to marry a certain respectable carpenter whom I know," he told the merchant. The merchant was overjoyed, for he had thought that the girl's talk about the carpenter had been the symptom, not the cause, of her disease. He had, in fact, thought her mad.

The traveller went to the carpenter, who built the pen for the goats. The goat-seller presented him with some fine animals; he took them to the goat-herd, who gave him goat-hair, which he took to the spinner, who gave him thread. Then he took the thread to the carpet-seller, who gave him a small carpet.

This carpet he carried back to the Sufi. When he arrived at the house of the wise man, the latter said to him: "Now I can give you knowledge; for you could not have brought this carpet unless you had worked for the carpet, and not for yourself."

Sources and Resources

AHSEN, AHKTER, *Eidetic Behavior.* Yonkers, N.Y. Eidetic Publishing House, 1973.

———*Basic Concepts in Eidetic Psychotherapy.* New York: Branden House, 1973.

AMERICAN SOCIETY for PSYCHICAL RESEARCH, "Courses and other Study Opportunities in Parapsychology," November 1974 (revised periodically), $2.00, 5 West 73rd Street, New York, N.Y. 10023.

ANASTASIOW, NICHOLAS, "Updating Intellectual Growth in Children and Bioplasmic Forces," *Phi Delta Kappan,* 55, no. 8, (April 1974), pp. 561-62.

ANDERSON, MARGARET, and RHEA WHITE, "ESP Score Level In Relation to Students' Attitude Toward Teacher-Agents Acting Simultaneously," *Journal of Parapsychology,* 22, pp. 20–28, 1958.

ARONS, HARRY, *Hypnosis for Speeding Up the Learning Process.* Irvington, N.J.: Power Publishers, Inc., 1974.

ASSAGIOLI, ROBERTO, "The Education of Gifted and Super-Gifted Children." New York: Psychosynthesis Research Foundation, 1960.

ASTOR, MARTIN, "Learning Through Hypnosis," *Educational Forum,* May 1971, pp. 447-55.

———"Transpersonal Approaches to Counseling," *Personnel and Guidance Journal,* 50, no. 2, pp. 801–8, 1972.

———"Transpersonal Counseling as a Form of Transcendental Education," *Counseling and Values,* 19, no. 2, (February, 1975), pp. 75–82.

BARLOW, W., "Psychosomatic Problems in Postural Re-education," *The Lancet,* September 24, 1955, pp. 659–64.

BERGER, E., "Zen Buddhism, General Psychology, and Counseling Psychology," *Journal of Counseling Psychology,* 9, (1962), pp. 122–127.

BIOFEEDBACK RESEARCH SOCIETY, *Biofeedback and Self-Regulation,* $6.50, Francine Butler, Executive Secretary, BRS, University of Colorado Medical College, C-268, 4200 E. Ninth Avenue, Denver, Colorado 80220. First published in 1973, contains a 113-page paperback of 800 references representing 850 authors.

BONNY, HELEN, *Creative Listening, Vol. 1: Music and Imagination Experiences for Children* (stereo record). Baltimore, Md.: Institute for Consciousness and Music, 1973.

BONNY, HELEN, *Creative Listening, Vol. 2: Dancing Around the World and Surprise Journey.* Baltimore, Md.: Institute for Consciousness and Music, 1975.

BONNY, HELEN and LOUIS SAVARY, *Music and Your Mind: Listening With a New Consciousness.* New York: Harper & Row, 1973.

BRUNER, JEROME, *On Knowing: Essays for the Left Hand.* New York: Atheneum, 1975.

CHRISTENSEN, J. A., "Cosmic Consciousness," *Media & Methods,* 11, no. 6, (February 1975), pp. 18–21.

CLARK, FRANCES V., "Rediscovering Transpersonal Education," *Journal of Transpersonal Psychology,* 6, no. 1, (1974), pp. 1–7.

———, "Fantasy and Imagination," in *Four Psychologies Applied to Education: Freudian, Behavioral, Humanistic, Transpersonal.* ed. T. B. Roberts, Cambridge, Mass.: Schenkman Publishing Co., 1975 C.

COLLIER, R. W., "The Effect of Transcendental Meditation Upon University Academic Attainment," Proceedings of the Pacific Northwest Conference on Foreign Languages, in press.

COUNSELING and VALUES, February 1975, whole number is on transpersonal counseling.

CRAMPTON, MARTHA, "Some Applications of Psychosynthesis in the Educational Field," speech before the Psychosynthesis Seminars 1971–72 series. Published by Psychosynthesis Research Foundation, New York, 1972. Also see entry 1975 C in this list for Thomas B. Roberts.

CRISWELL, ELEANOR, "Experimental Yoga Course for College Students: A Progress Report," *Journal of Transpersonal Psychology,* 2, no. 1, (1970), pp. 71–78.

DANSKIN, D. G., and E. D. WALTERS, "Biofeedback and Voluntary Self-Regulation Counseling and Education," *Personnel and Guidance Journal,* 51, no. 9, (1973), pp. 633–638.

———, "Biofeedback Training as Counseling," *Counseling and Values,* 19, no. 2, (February 1975), pp. 116–22.

DILLEY, JOSIAH S., "Mental Imagery," *Counseling and Values,* 19, no. 2, (February 1975), pp. 110–15.

DOWNING, GEORGE, *The Massage Book.* Berkeley: Bookworks (distributed by Random House), 1972.

DOWNING, JACK, *Dreams and Nightmares.* New York: Harper & Row, 1973.

DRISCOLL, FRANCIS, "TM as a Secondary School Subject," *Phi Delta Kappan,* 54, no. 4, (December 1972), pp. 236–37. Also see entry 1975 C in this list for Thomas B. Roberts.

EGAN, RICHARD M. and WILLIAM, "The Effect of Hypnosis on Academic Performance," *The American Journal of Clinical Hypnosis,* (July 1968), pp. 31–34.

EHRENWALD, JAN, "The Occult," *Today's Education,* 60, no. 6 (September 1971), 28-30.

ELLIOT, JAMES, "ESP and Relaxation," *Personal Growth,* no. 21 (1974), pp. 13–17, P. O. Box 1254, Berkeley, Calif. 94701.

EVANS-WENTZ, W., *Tibetan Yoga and Secret Doctrines.* New York: Oxford University Press, 1935.

FARADAY, ANNE., *Dream Power.* New York: Coward, McCann & Geoghegan, 1972.

———, *The Dream Game.* New York: Coward, McCann & Geoghegan, 1975.

FELDENKRAIS, MOSHE, *Awareness Through Movement*. New York: Harper & Row, 1972.

————, *Body and Mature Behavior*. New York: International Universities Press, 1970.

FENG, GIA-FU and H. WILKERSON, *Tai-Chi: A Way of Centering*. New York: Macmillan, Collier Books, 1969.

FREYBERG, JOAN T., "Increasing Children's Fantasies: Hold High the Card-board Sword," *Psychology Today*, 8, no. 9 (February 1975), pp. 63–64, 120.

Fundamentals of Progress: Scientific Research on Transcendental Meditation. Los Angeles: Maharishi International University, 1974.

GALLWEY, W. TIMOTHY, *The Inner Game of Tennis*. New York: Random House, 1974.

GOLAS, THADDEUS, *The Lazy Man's Guide to Enlightenment*. Palo Alto: The Seed Center, 1972.

GOVINDA, LAMA, *Way of the White Cloud*. Berkeley: Shambala Publications, 1971.

GREEN, ELMER E., ALYCE M. GREEN, E. DALE WALTERS, "Voluntary Control of Internal States: Psychological and Physiological," *The Journal of Trans-personal Psychology*, 2, no. 1, (1970), pp. 1–26.

GREEN, ELMER E., and ALYCE M, "The Ins and Outs of Mind-Body Energy," *Science Year, 1974: World Book Science Annual*, Chicago: Field Enterprises Educational Corp., 1974. Also in Roberts, 1975.

GUNTHER, BERNARD, *Sense Relaxation*. New York: Macmillan, Collier Books, 1968.

HAIGHT, M., and G. JAMPOLSKY, "An Experience with Biofeedback in a Public High School," *Journal of Bio-feedback*, (Winter 1974).

HEATON, D. P., and D. ORME-JOHNSON, "Influence of Transcendental Medita-tion on Grade Point Average: Initial Findings," in Orme-Johnson, D. W. L. Dumash, and J. Farrow (eds.), *Scientific Research on Transcendental Medita-tion: Collected Papers & Vol. I*. Los Angeles: Maharishi International Uni-versity Press, 1975.

HENDRICKS, GAY, and RUSSEL WILLS, *The Centering Book: Awareness Activities for Children, Parents, and Teachers*. Englewood Cliffs, N.J.: Prentice-Hall, Inc., Spectrum Books, 1975.

HIGGINS, JAMES E., *Mystical Fancy in Children's Literature*. New York: Teacher's College Press, Columbia University, 1970.

HOLT, JOHN, *Escape from Childhood*. New York: E. P. Dutton, 1974.

HOUSTON, JEAN, "Putting the First Man on Earth," *Saturday Review*, February 22, 1975, pp. 28–32, 53.

HUANG, AL, *Embrace Tiger, Return to Mountain*. Moab, Utah: Real People Press, 1973.

HUXLEY, ALDOUS, "Education on the Nonverbal Level," *Daedalus*, Spring 1962. Also in *Contemporary Educational Psychology*, ed. Richard M. Jones. New York: Harper & Row, 1967.

————, Introduction to *The Perennial Philosophy* Cleveland: World Publishing Co., Meridan Books, pp. iv–viii, 1968.

————, *Island.* New York: Harper & Row, 1972.

IYENGAR, B. K. S., *Light on Yoga.* New York: Schocken Books, 1966.

JACOBSON, E. O., *You Must Relax.* New York: McGraw-Hill, 1957.

————, *Anxiety and Tension Control.* Philadelphia: Lippincott, 1964.

JONES, RICHARD M., "Involving Fantasies and Feelings," in *Facts and Feelings in the Classroom,* Louis J. Rubin. New York: Viking, Compass Books, 1973, pp. 171-92.

KANELLAKOS, DEMETRI P., *The Psychobiology of Transcendental Meditation: An Annotated Bibliography,* Los Angeles: Maharishi International University, Spring 1973.

KANTOR, ROBERT, "The Affective Domain and Beyond," *Journal for the Study of Consciousness,* 3, no. 1 (January–June 1970), pp. 20–42. Also in Roberts, 1975 C.

KATZ, RICHARD, "Education for Transcendence," in *Preludes for Growth,* pp. 206–24. New York: Free Press, 1973.

KELEMAN, STANLEY, *Bio-Energetic Concepts of Grounding.* San Francisco: Lodestar Press, 1970.

KENNETT, JIYU, *Selling Water by the River.* New York: Random House, Vintage Books, 1972.

KRIPPNER, STANLEY, "Parapsychology and Education," *Journal of Humanistic Psychology,* 13, no. 4 (Fall 1973), pp. 17-20. Excerpt from "Humanistic Psychology and Parapsychology," pp. 3-24. Also in Roberts, 1975 C.

KRISHNAMURTI, JIDDU, *Education and the Significance of Life.* New York: Harper & Row, 1953.

LAGERWERFF, E. B., and K. A. PERLROTH MENSENDIECK, *Your Posture and Your Pain.* Garden City, New York: Doubleday, Anchor Books, 1973.

LANGFORD, CRICKET, *Meditation for Little People.* Novato, Calif.: Inner Light Foundation, 1974.

LEONARD, GEORGE, "The Human Potential," in *Education and Ecstasy,* Chapter 2, pp. 23–50. New York: Delacorte Press, 1968.

LESH, TERRY V., "Zen Meditation and the Development of Empathy in Counselors," *Journal of Humanistic Psychology,* 10, no. 1 (Spring 1970), pp. 39-74. Also in Roberts, 1975 C.

LESHAN, LAWRENCE, *How To Meditate: A Guide to Self-Discovery.* Boston: Little, Brown, 1974.

————, *The Medium, The Mystic, and the Physicist.* New York: Random House, Ballantine Books, 1975.

LINDEN, WILLIAM, "The Relation Between the Practice of Meditation by School Children and Their Levels of Field Dependence-Independence, Text Anxiety and Reading Achievement," *Journal of Consulting and Clinical Psychology,* 41, no. 1, (August 1973), pp. 139–43.

LOWEN, ALEXANDER, *The Betrayal of the Body.* New York: Macmillan, 1967.

LUCE, GAY G., *Body Time*. New York: Pantheon, 1971.

LUK, C., *The Secrets of Chinese Meditation*. London: Rider, 1964.

MCCONNELL, R. A., "ESP and Credibility in Science" *The American Psychologist*, 24, (1969), pp. 531–38.

MCKIM, ROBERT H., *Experiences in Visual Thinking*, ERIC, ED-073-690. Monterey, Calif: Brooks/Cole, 1972.

MASLOW, ABRAHAM, "Lessons From the Peak-Experiences," *Journal of Humanistic Psychology*, 2, no. 2, (1962), pp. 9–18.

———, *The Farther Reaches of Human Nature*. New York: Viking, 1971.

MASTERS, ROBERT., and J. HOUSTON, *Mind Games*. New York: Viking, 1972.

MAUPIN, EDWARD W., "Zen Buddhism: A Psychological Review," *Journal of Counseling Psychology*, 26, (1962), pp. 362–78, No month of publication available.

MORRIS, FREIDA, *Self-Hypnosis in Two Days*. Berkeley: Intergalactic Publishing Co., 1974.

MURPHY, MICHAEL, "Education for Transcendence," *Journal of Transpersonal Psychology*, 1, no. 1, (Spring 1969), pp. 21–32. Also in Roberts, 1975.

———, *Golf in the Kingdom*. New York: Viking, 1972.

MUSES, CHARLES, "Taint Necessarily So: A New Look at Education," *Journal for the Study of Consciousness*, 4, no. 2, (1971), pp. 101–4.

NARANJO, CLAUDIO, "The Oneness of Experience in the Ways of Growth," from *The One Quest*, pp. 123–28. New York: Viking, 1973.

NARANJO, CLAUDIO, and ROBERT ORNSTEIN, *On The Psychology of Meditation*. New York: Viking, 1971.

NORDBERG, R. B., *The Teenager and the New Mysticism*. New York: Richards Rosen Press, 1973.

———, "Paths to Mysticism in the 1970's," *Counseling and Values*, 17, no. 3, (1973), pp. 167–75.

———, "Meditation: Future Vehicle for Career Exploration," *Vocational Guidance Quarterly*, 22, (June 1974), 267–71.

———, "Mysticism—Its Implications for Helping Relationships," *Counseling and Values*, 19, no. 2, (February 1975), pp. 99–109.

OGLETREE, EARL J., "Rudolf Steiner: Unknown Educator," *Elementary School Journal*, 74, no. 6, (March 1974), pp. 344–52.

ORME-JOHNSON, D. W., L. DOMASH, and J. FARROW (eds), *Scientific Research on Transcendental Meditation: Collected Papers, Vol. 1*. Los Angeles: Maharishi International University Press, 1975.

ORNSTEIN, ROBERT E., "The Education of the Intuitive Mode," in *The Psychology of Consciousness*. Chapter 7, pp. 143–79, San Francisco: W. H. Freeman, 1972.

OSTRANDER, SHIELA, and LYNN SCHROEDER, "Artificial Reincarnation," in *Psychic Discoveries Behind the Iron Curtain*, Chapter 12, pp. 146–59, New York: Bantam Books, 1971. Also in Roberts, 1975 C.

PEARCE, JOSEPH, *The Crack in the Cosmic Egg.* New York: Simon & Schuster, Pocket Books, 1973.

———, *Exploring the Crack in the Cosmic Egg,* New York: Julian Press, 1974.

PEERBOLTE, M., "Meditation for School Children," *Main Currents in Modern Thought,* 24, (1967), pp. 19–21.

PIAGET, JEAN, *The Construction of Reality in the Child.* New York: Ballantine, 1954.

PULVINO, CHARLES J., and JAMES L. LEE, "Counseling According to Don Juan," *Counseling and Values,* 19, no. 2, (February 1975), pp. 125–30.

RAPPAPORT, BERNARD S., "Carnal Knowledge: What the Wisdom of the Body Has to Offer Psychotherapy," *Journal of Humanistic Psychology,* 15, no. 1 (Winter 1975), pp. 49–70.

REPS, PAUL, *Be! New Uses for the Human Instrument.* New York: Weatherhill, 1971.

RICHARD, MICHAEL, "Attention Training: A Pilot Program in the Development of Autonomic Control," *Contemporary Education,* 43, no. 3, (January 1972), pp. 57–60.

RICHARDS, MARY C., *Centering.* Middletown, Conn.: Wesleyan University Press, 1969.

ROBERTS, THOMAS B., "Transpersonal: The New Educational Psychology," *Phi Delta Kappan,* (November 1974), pp. 191–93.

———, *Transpersonal: The New Educational Psychology,* ERIC ED-099-252, April 1975 A.

ROBERTS, THOMAS B. (ed)., "Transpersonal Psychology Applied to Education," Section IV of *Four Psychologies Applied to Education,* pp. 392–550. Cambridge, Mass.: Schenkman Publishing Co., 1975 C.

ROBERTS, THOMAS B., and FRANCES V. CLARK, *Transpersonal Psychology in Education,* Fastback Pamphlet Series #53 (April 1975). Bloomington, Ind.: Phi Delta Kappa Educational Foundation. B.

ROLF, IDA P., "Structural Integration," *Journal of the Institute for the Comparative Study of History, Philosophy and the Sciences,* 1, no. 1 (June 1963), pp. 56–57.

SAMPLES, ROBERT E., "Kari's Handicap: The Impediment of Creativity," *The Saturday Review,* July 1967, pp. 56–57.

———, *Opening: A Primer for Self-Actualization,* Menlo Park, Calif.: Addison-Wesley, 1973.

———, "Learning With the Whole Brain," *Human Behavior,* 4, (February 1975), pp. 16–23, 79.

———, "Are You Teaching Only One Side of the Brain?", *Learning,* (February 1975), pp. 25–28.

SAMUELS, MICHAEL., and HAL BENNETT, *The Well Body Book.* New York: Random House, 1973.

SATURDAY REVIEW, February 22, 1975. The entire issue is devoted to transpersonal psychology.

SCHULTZ, J. H., and W. LUTHE, *Autogenic Training: A Psychophysiological Approach to Psychotherapy.* New York: Grune & Stratton, 1959.

SEEMAN, WILLIAM, SANFORD, NIDICH, and THOMAS BANTA, "Influence of Transcendental Meditation on a Measure of Self-Actualization," *Journal of Counseling Psychology,* 19, no. 3, (1972), pp. 184–187.

SHAH, IDRIES., *Caravan of Dreams.* London: Octagon Press, 1968.

———, *The Pleasantries of the Incredible Mulla Nasrudin.* London: Jonathan Cape, 1968.

———, *The Dermis Probe.* London: Jonathan Cape, 1970.

SINGER, JEROME, *Daydreaming.* New York: Random House, 1966.

SKOVHOLT, T. M., and R. W. HOENNINGER, "Guided Fantasy in Career Counseling," *Personnel and Guidance Journal,* 52, no. 10, (1974), pp. 693–96.

SOBEL, DAVID, and F. HORNBACHER, *An Everyday Guide to Your Health.* New York: Grossman Publishers, 1973.

SPOLIN, VIOLA, *Improvisations for the Theatre.* Evanston, Ill.: Northwestern University Press, 1963.

TRUNGPA, C., *Meditation in Action.* Berkeley: Shambala Publications, 1969.

WEIL, ANDREW, *The Natural Mind: A New Way of Looking at Drugs and the Higher Consciousness,* pp. 19–25 and 30–37, Boston: Houghton Mifflin, 1972.

WHITE, JOHN (ed.), *What Is Meditation?* Garden City, N.Y.: Doubleday, Anchor Books, 1974.

WOLPE, J., and A. LAZARUS, *Behavior Therapy Techniques.* Long Island City, N.Y.: Pergamon Press, 1966.

WOODS, RALPH L., and HERBERT B. GREENHOUSE, *The New World of Dreams.* New York: Macmillan, 1974.

ZIEGENFUSS, BEATRICE W., "Hypnosis: A Tool for Education," *Education,* (April 1962), pp. 505–7.